Andrea M. Cross 1977-

No Fear of Winter: Wrapped in His Strength

ISBN: 978-0-9756395-0-4

1. Devotional 2. Bible Study 3. Christian Discipleship

DISCLAIMER:

Cover picture by J Pelino. Used with permission under license from Canva.

Printed in Australia
PUBLISHED BY ANDREA CROSS
Vermont South, VICTORIA 3977
andrea@gozoe.org

WRAPPED IN HIS STRENGTH

NO FEAR OF WINTER

WHEN THREATEDNED, HE DEFENDS ME.
WHEN WEAK, HE IS STRONG.
WHEN LONELY, HE HOLDS ME CLOSE.

Contents

Acknowledgments

First I want to both acknowledge and bring glory to God through this book. He is my provider, comforter, ever present Help in times of need, healer and Heavenly Father. I am nothing without Him. He is with me through every trial and I could not go on without Him. Blessed be Your name Lord God.

To my husband David. You are so amazing. I don't even know how to describe how helpful, supportive, understanding, patient and encouraging you are. You continue to smile sweetly and stop what *you're* doing to help me with my "ideas," even when you have your own work to complete. Thanks for never giving up on me!

To my three precious children, Tobiah, Eliana and Spencer. I know it was not your choice to move so far away from your grandparents, cousins and extended family but you have accepted this call from God on our family with grace and love. I marvel at your ability to adapt and change. You have graciously allowed me to tell your stories so that many others can walk alongside us on this journey. You have given people a glimpse as to how great our God is, how faithfully He provides and how amazing His love. Thanks also for continuously reminding me of how blessed I am to be a mum and for making me smile!

To Ron Boyer. I know you probably wouldn't *want* to be mentioned but you have always been so willing to read my work and have been a great source of encouragement to me - thank you!

And finally, to my parents. I am overwhelmed. How do I describe what you mean to me? How could I ever put into words the support, the prayers, the love, the encouragement, the tenderness that abounds in you both? What a joy it is to be your daughter. I am continually reminded of how rare it is to have been brought up without divorce, abuse or neglect. You have taught me so much. Dad, this book would still be sitting in my computer if it wasn't for your tireless follow-ups and practical support these past couple of years. Thank you!

-SEASONS-

Life cycles round in circles,
a change each season sends
An ever-turning spiral,
no beginning and no end.
From autumn
through to winter
from spring to summertime,
Keep waiting
and you'll find again
the sun will start to shine!

-AUTHOR UNKNOWN-

Hello

I stand in my kitchen with sweat dripping down my back. It is just another ordinary afternoon in Northern Thailand, the fan doing nothing but blowing hot air on me. And although I feel drenched with perspiration (again) I really am grateful not to be cold. I don't like wintry weather at all.

The small, enclosed kitchen where I wait for inspiration to decide what to cook for dinner provides a home for mixing bowls, appliances, jars of spices, and all manner of nuts, seeds and beans. It's the epicenter of our home, serving up countless meals for hungry teenagers, as well as healthy snacks, cakes and little jars of chocolate mousse. These treats are for the days we celebrate, commiserate or just need a little extra something. This place is where I spend a lot of my time not only cooking, but also pondering life.

Let me say that I'm so glad you're here. Not literally in my kitchen with me, but ready to embark on this journey of reflection. The circumstances or 'moments' in life that help to prepare, nourish, prune and grow us into all we were created to be, are scattered throughout the seasons of life. It has been restorative for me to see how the snippets of my life are intertwining together to reveal a tapestry in the making. It might look like a mess right now, but I know God is making something beautiful out of these raggedy, colourful threads.

My friends all think I love to cook, but I don't really. I love to nourish. I love to make sure that my family not only leaves the table full, but that they eat all the right foods that will sustain, energise, fight off infection and help them to grow. But most importantly my goal, each time we gather around the table, is that we also nourish our spirits. Thinking of new ways to cook using the same ingredients night after night is not only about being creative, but it's also about an opportunity to deeply impact those gathered right in front of us. It is a matter of understanding that it's not 'just' dinner. It's about designing a menu that includes being grateful, sharing devotions together, reflecting on the goodness of God and spurring each other on towards love and good deeds. By the time my children leave our home, my desire is that they'll not only know how to create amazing, nutritious meals for themselves, but that they'll have a healthy and nourishing spiritual relationship with their Creator as well.

So, while this book is mainly about life, you'll also find that some of our family recipes have crept in here too. Now you can sit and feed both your body and soul as you read, using the questions at the end of each section to reflect on your own life. So please make yourself at home by grabbing a coffee or a snack and get ready to nourish yourself through the pages of this book.

Seasons

I grew up in Melbourne a.k.a. 'four-seasons-in-one-day.' The seasons I knew followed in turn, summer-autumn-winter-spring, year after year. They brought with them waves of familiarity from plum picking in backyard trees, open fires on cold nights, long woolen school socks and taking swimming lessons at the local outdoor pool. Those 'things' that I remember in each season, I came to accept, and expect as being normal and wonderful — despite how inconvenient or uncomfortable they may have been.

Seasons for me now are so very different. And interestingly, by comparison, my children are growing up in an entirely different hemisphere, where even the *number* of seasons in the year is not the same! Wherever you live in the world, you'll know that the beginning of each season is not just acknowledged by looking at the date on the calendar, but by the signs that mark the end of the season before it. Leaves falling from the trees, snow melting away, longer days, the first rain, the smell of a certain tree, cooler mornings ... whatever those signs are, there is a certain rhythm to the seasons and an understanding of what to expect. After living in Thailand for many years, there is a sequence and a pattern to the three seasons here that I have now become used to.

Life progresses with a certain rhythm too. If your life is anything like mine though, it usually feels less like the steady beat of a metronome and much more unpredictable ... even beating out-of-control at times.

By sharing anecdotes from *my* family and *my* journey, I desire to communicate that even when the seasons change, God's love remains the same. If we know His love then we can laugh at the storm, remain upright through the winds as well as love whatever season we find ourselves in, all because of this one constant — His presence and strength in our lives.

One night, when I was praying about an issue in our family and crying out to God for help, a verse from Proverbs 31 came to my mind. It was not until the next day that I suddenly knew what the name for this book would be. Around that time our family was enduring a very difficult season — a long, bitter winter so to speak. As I was reflecting on how we were coming through, what we'd learnt and what advice I would give to someone else who was struggling, I was drawn to this verse.

The virtuous woman has no fear for the coming winters because her family was covered in fine, expensive clothing suitable for winter. Her household was well stocked for times of need. (Paraphrased)

I read somewhere once that 'strength doesn't always look and feel like you think it will.' Sometimes strength is walking away from a harsh comment that you know was spoken by a hurting person, sometimes it's seen in the tears that cry out, *'Lord, I need you'*; and other times strength is just surviving the day without being overly critical of yourself, remembering that you're doing the best that you can.

So, I began to question, how was it possible for this virtuous, honorable woman in Proverbs 31 to have no fear of winter? I believe it was because she knew her family was 'covered' in their time of need. And then it dawned on me, that if there was one thing I had felt so strongly throughout that wintry season, it was that God had protected our family. There's no earthly person who could've taken better care of us. When I put my trust completely in Him, I see my household provided for abundantly. When I feel threatened, He defends me. When I am weak, He is strong. When I experience loneliness, He holds me close. *This* is my testimony!

Our struggles in that season may not turn out to be the coldest winter our family will ever have to endure, but because of His covering, I don't have to fear the winds, the snow or the cold spells that will come at us in the future. I love how Psalm 23:6 is written in The Passion Translation, *"So why would I fear the future? For your goodness and love pursue me all the days of my life. Then afterward when my life is through, I'll return to your glorious presence to be forever with you!"* Praising God in the hard seasons is the way to feel His presence in every season. It is a constant, conscious decision to worship intentionally regardless of the circumstances, or whatever the season we find ourselves in.

I invite you to come with me on a journey through the seasons of *my* life and be encouraged to embrace every season of your own ... yes, even winter!

Andrea

Hello Summer

'God uses this season to draw us back into His arms.'

I close my eyes remembering hanging upside down on our A-framed 1980's swing set, jumping on the trampoline, climbing trees, and playfully frolicking under the sprinkler in the front yard. The smell of barbeques, the feeling of running barefoot on the lawn (dodging bees) and hearing the melodic chimes of *Mister Whippy's* ice-cream van, as he came down the big hill and passed our house. These wonderful moments are just some of the summer memories that come flooding back to my mind growing up in Melbourne, Australia. Summer just so happened to be my favourite season as a child. I loved its warmth and felt most alive when the sun was shining down on me.

Born in 1977, the second child of three, my parents loved me well. Through the summers, my olive skin would glow with a deep tan. I loved being outdoors. My long dark hair contrasted with my light blue eyes, which were always sparkling with adventurous ideas. I was never bored. There was always a world of new ideas waiting — new obstacle courses to be built in the backyard, cubby houses to make, trampoline challenges or even swinging round on the rotary clothesline. The pleasures of icy-poles, playing outside, or simply being squirted by the hose have left lasting impressions on me to this day. The simplicity of life back then still echoes sweet reminders of the way life used to be so ... uncomplicated!

Aside from just the physical attributes of summertime, there are many words that describe the personal 'summers' in my life. The pleasurable aspects of the summer seasons include celebrations, new adventures, travel, promotions, excitement, productivity and gaining confidence. Running parallel though, have been times where the summer seemed almost unbearable. Life's circumstances reached 'boiling point,' 'drought' or experienced a 'heat wave.' The warmth was no longer enjoyable, everything felt chaotic. It was as though a major case of heatstroke, sunburn and dehydration left me feeling confused, exhausted and alone in the desert.

Throughout the scorching heat — the summers in my life have been seasons of extremes. They have encompassed joy-filled times, passion, excitement and moments of deep gratitude and reflection. There have been times of thankfulness for summer showers, rainbows, eating berries and staying outdoors longer during the daylight savings hours. But they have also seen the need to be watered (even soaked at times) when my spirit felt as dry as the air, and when indifference, sluggishness and lack of enthusiasm have crept in. When I have metaphorically sat in the blazing heat of the day, stubbornly gripping to the hope that I would see God answer my prayers, I have had to hold onto His promises and fully trust in who He says He is.

Exhausted

Back in December, the summer of 2009, my husband David and I prepared to move our family to Thailand. There were many apprehensive thoughts running through my mind, but the sense of excitement and adventure seemed to balance out the anxiety that I was internalising. Realistically, I didn't expect to find the move to a developing nation particularly easy with three children (the eldest being only four years old). Having never lived outside of Melbourne, my adventurous spirit kept my thoughts optimistic about all that was about to transpire and the rapidly approaching departure date.

Before we left, I started to imagine what cooking in a new country, driving in different conditions, speaking a foreign language and adjusting to a hot, tropical climate might be like. As my thoughts whirled with self-doubt about how these things might actually be really challenging for me, my positive thoughts assured me that it couldn't really be that bad! *Could it?!*

If I am truly being honest though, I must admit that, in that first year, 'culture shock' hit me in a way that I never saw coming. It wasn't the food, the driving, the language or the weather that affected me the most, although, don't get me wrong, all those new ways of living were hard to adapt to. No, the aspect of moving to a completely different part of the world that I reacted to the most was the impact of the sudden loss of my community, family and friends.

I thought I was emotionally prepared. I totally expected that I'd miss people, but I never anticipated it would hit me quite so hard as it did. Honestly it took me some time to accept that, for the first time in my life — amongst a population of sixty-five million other people — I felt lonely. *Really* lonely!

When we arrived in Chiang Mai in January 2010, it was such a whirlwind of activity; trying to buy a car, find items for the house, get a driver's license ... the list was long! We had shipped some boxes earlier that were meant to arrive in Thailand at the same time we would. These boxes held precious items to make the children's bedrooms feel familiar. They contained towels and cutlery — lots of homewares that would save us having to buy so many new things. That was the plan anyway, until we were informed that our boxes were temporarily misplaced. They were last seen in Singapore but no one knew where they were, or when they'd arrive. This added more to our 'to do' list and each day we went through a mixture of emotions from unmet expectations, frustration, confusion and exhaustion.

The exhaustion is hard to explain. It wasn't jet lag or normal tiredness — I was getting enough sleep. But part of the culture shock I felt included feeling overwhelmed by even the smallest problems. Even my decision-making skills seemed to be affected. Before I left Australia, my behaviour, body language, and social cues were automatic and required little to no attention. Moving to a new country though, a heightened sense of awareness kicked in because these things were so unfamiliar and oftentimes confusing.

I remember when I was pregnant, in that first trimester, I felt an extreme fatigue like nothing else I had ever experienced before. It was not the same as staying up during university years studying for exams or pulling off an 'all-nighter' to get an assignment finished. It wasn't like having multiple late nights finishing reports as a teacher and then having to teach the next day. Or how you feel on New Year's day after a big party. It was different. Insane!

When we moved to Thailand, I felt this dreadful tiredness again. After long, hot days trying to solve issues, pay bills, return faulty items, or even just finding where to purchase something that *seemed* relatively simple. We would then go through the crazy dinner hour with preschoolers reacting to different-tasting foods and dealing with their own emotions only to end each long day by trying to settle three, apprehensive, young children into unfamiliar beds and begin language lessons from 8-10 pm Incidentally, the night-time-language-classes-idea didn't last very long before I collapsed in an uncontrollable fit of tears. It was just too much. It would be a whole year before I could try formal language learning again, and an area that I continued to struggle with.

Community

It seems strange to write it down, and I'm not quite sure how it happened, but somewhere during the months leading up to arriving in Thailand, I had become caught up in the idea of finally getting to serve and help at the ZOE Children's Home; that I'd momentarily overlooked the fact that we had three small children of our own that still needed caring for.

The more we settled into our new home, the more excitedly I wondered how God was going to use me in Thailand.

One month after arriving, I was invited to attend a women's conference for Thai and foreign Christian workers. I was anticipating that God might speak to me at the conference ... but what He said was not at all what I was expecting to hear!

The speaker had almost finished sharing when she called up those women who wanted prayer for a particular reason to come forward. It wasn't something that was relevant to me, so I remained in my seat but most of the other women made their way to the front. I was sitting on my chair, head bowed, praying quietly alone when I felt a tap on my shoulder. It was a missionary lady. As I looked up, I saw that besides her and me, most of the other women were praying up front near the pulpit. *"I think God wants me to share something with you ... "* she began. I knew it! This was what I had been anticipating. My future position revealed ... my assignment ... I couldn't wait to hear what God wanted me to do! I was so excited. That was until she said, *"Your ministry in this season is with your children at home, along with supporting your husband. Your family needs you most right now. You can try to do other things but you will be doing them in your own strength."* I was gutted. I turned back around in my seat and put my head into my hands and cried. And then it occurred to me that I wouldn't actually be 'going off to work' with my husband when he started but continuing the job of looking after our children ... at home. Alone!

When I got home and shared with David what had happened, he asked me what I was going to do. As hard as it was to accept that I wouldn't be 'working' I told him, "I didn't move halfway across the world to disobey God. I will trust that He knows what is best for our family." (And, as it turned out, He did.) God was so faithful in that season. Without committing to any formal job role in those early years, He still sweetly blessed me with many opportunities to join in activities at ZOE with our children, be included in future planning, spend time with short term teams and form relationships with the other mothers on the mission field.

It was still with a little jealousy that I waved goodbye to David as he departed for his first day working at ZOE, but I knew that God was in charge and that He would show me when the right time to begin work outside the home would be. Once Dave started working, I suddenly found myself not only in an unfamiliar country with no language acquisition, and very limited cultural awareness; but I also felt very much alone during the long hot days at home. After the sudden loss of my community, family and friends I tried hard to imagine where I would 'fit' in and if I'd ever find a community like the one I had in Australia.

There's so much to be learned from trees. Did you know that environmental factors can cause a tree to become stressed? Just like with people, trees are also affected by negative influences like drought, overcrowding and damage to their roots (their anchors) and even the loss of other trees! I read this interesting statement from Peter Wohlleben, a German forester, who said "When trees grow together, nutrients and water can be optimally divided among them all so that each tree can grow into the best tree it can be. If you 'help' individual trees by getting rid of their supposed competition, the remaining trees are bereft. They send messages out to their neighbors in vain because nothing remains but stumps. Every tree now muddles along on its own, giving rise to great differences in productivity ... because a tree can be only as strong as the forest that surrounds it."

Warburton is located in the famous Yarra Valley, 1.5 hours east of Melbourne. Located a few kilometres outside of Warburton is a forest of Californian Redwoods, Sequoia sempervirens which I am determined to visit one year when I visit Melbourne. It had been on my bucket list for a while now,* and I had appreciated the many videos and photos I'd seen, but I couldn't wait to see a giant sequoia or California redwood for myself. As the tallest trees in the world, they're known to be both majestic and strong. Reaching up toward heaven, I've read that they can withstand harsh winds, earthquakes and even storms.

*(NOTE: This goal was achieved in 2022.)

There are so many interesting facts about these gigantic trees. First, they defy gravity with their ability to carry water to their highest points. Their thick bark, with deep grooves, gives them a fire-resistant characteristic; and research shows that older trees are actually able to survive fires because their bark is so thick it acts like a fireproof shell. Yet, it's not the height or the strength of these trees that most intrigues me ... it's their root system!

You'd imagine these trees must have a root system that reaches really far down to be able to support their height and weight, but strangely they don't. These trees actually have a relatively shallow, horizontal root system that extends over one hundred feet (thirty metres) from the base. What's interesting about them is that they intertwine their roots with the roots of the other redwoods. This increases their stability during strong winds and floods. Their roots only go down two to three metres and yet, what is so amazing is that because they are all linked together, these trees rarely fall over.

What's also interesting about redwoods is that they don't survive alone. They form 'tribes' or communities. Sometimes they grow so close to each other, they merge at the base into one tree. They provide each other with strength and support by their intertwining roots, living in the embrace of others. Their merged roots also meet their need for nurture. The entire root system relies on connections ... an underground network of powerful bonds. To me, redwoods are a beautiful representation of 'community.' They embody exactly what it's all about — interdependence.

In those early months and years of transition, I felt a bit like a redwood that had suddenly become detached from the wonderful, extensive root system in which it had once been intertwined. I was separated from the community that I had been strengthened by and there I stood all alone, transplanted in another area without the stability or the nurture of the interwoven root system I had previously known.

Feeling vulnerable, I wondered what to do without my 'tribe' and community. With whom would I 'knot' my roots with now? Could I still stand strong against fires or floods that threatened to destroy?

Connections

After about seven years of being married, we decided to start a family. Our desire was to have our children close in age but of course we were unsure how long it would take to fall pregnant or if having multiple births close together was even possible. So, after our three children were all born within just over three years of each other, my hands and my heart were full with a tribe of precious little people. I chose to stay at home during this time and not return to my job as a teacher. Dave and I had travelled to many different countries before settling down to start a family and I felt content with our comfortable life in Australia. It was such a joy and pleasure to be at home with my babies full-time, and I was so thankful that finances were not a reason for us to worry about the loss of my income. Although there were days when it was rough, or I felt unqualified in my new role, I viewed the challenges of potty training, infant illnesses or two-year-old tantrums as nothing more than temporary setbacks, which I navigated my way through and moved on. I found myself overwhelmingly content as the mother of three beautiful healthy children.

As time passed though, I looked around and realised that the positive transition that I had made to become a mother, was not the same for everyone else. I knew friends who were experiencing postnatal depression, feelings of loneliness, uncertainty and exhaustion — wondering if they could fully adjust to their new role as somebody's mother. The shift from once having a notable career to now wiping bottoms and cleaning up vomit was more drastic than they'd anticipated ... and it left them questioning whether there was ever going to be more to life than 'just' being a mum.

I wondered what I could do to support these precious women around me. And so, the idea for a support group was conceived. It was a concept totally focused on encouraging mothers through coffee meet-ups and online support materials. Once a month those who could meet would gather together and have morning tea and share life. I would provide a newsletter written about a particular parenting issue and give a small gift of encouragement. I believed that if I could help empower mothers, then their children, families and the broader community would be affected in positive ways. I wanted these mums to feel acknowledged in their role, reassured, inspired and (at the very least) hopeful. I knew that being a mum was hard work but I also knew how powerful it could be to regain perspective by simply getting together, chatting over a cup of coffee and having someone to connect, share, relax, relate to and recharge with.

During this time, I discovered the enjoyment of researching different topics and writing monthly newsletters. I began posting the newsletters on a blog called 'Loving Mums' so that even if mothers weren't able to make the meet up, they could still feel encouraged and connected. The more that I wrote, the more I realised that this was something that I found both relaxing and enjoyable. And whilst I would feel disappointed when the attendance was low for some reason, I knew that if the group had helped to support at least one mother, that it was all worth it. Unbeknownst to me, when I started the group, was how much I would benefit from it myself. I loved writing the newsletters and meeting up with other mums. Starting a group was something I never thought I'd do but it stretched me, it taught me lots about myself and it helped me to understand more about the important task of raising children and what a challenge that can be at times.

As I look back on this time, one thing I recognise learning more about, was hearing God's voice and trusting in Him. These lessons have stayed with me over the years that I have lived in Thailand and they were essential in those first few months of feeling alone. So many times, I have not been able to see the answer to a situation right away, but I can rely on the knowledge that God will come through! It may not be in my timing, it may not be how I expect but I know He will always answer my prayers.

During that first season in Thailand of preschool drop-offs, nap times and trying to entertain an active toddler in over 40-degree heat when the air was polluted, or the electricity went out, I realised pretty quickly that I had no choice but to rely on God. I was very aware of the sudden absence of the 'community' that I had before. It hit me hard when the reality set in of not having my mother and sister close by, my mother's group, Mainly Music morning, MOPS, swimming lessons, my walking partners or the community mothers' group that I had started up. I went from having an abundance of close friends to being 'that mother' — the *one* I'd tried to help. The *one* who didn't know anybody else. The *one* who needed the extra support.

Feeling overwhelmed, I struggled through meeting people briefly at preschool drop-offs. Each encounter was exhausting. As I'd exchange details and background information with new acquaintances, I yearned for catchups with my mum, sister or my dearest friends who knew me. I longed for a conversation that didn't start with, "So, how long have you been here?" and ended with "And how long will you stay?" I ached just to be 'known' again.

It's hard to describe it in words but in those early months, I started to feel like I was losing myself. I questioned: *"Who was I ... now that life looked so different? Who was I ... now that everything and everyone I'd known had been stripped away? Who was I ... in this foreign place? Now that I had to explain and introduce myself all the time ... who was I?"*

It's a question that I have had to unpack and discover the answer to over many years. I needed a deep and genuine understanding that regardless of anything else, I knew who I was and *Whose* I was. But back then, I came to learn that even though I had been expecting the transition to be hard, there was no preparation for how difficult it actually was. Whether it's culture shock, or a different kind of change, these seasons can be brutal. It's easy to get discouraged. It's easy to feel overwhelmed. It's easy to feel alone.

Steve Cole, a genomics researcher at the University of California, Los Angeles said, *"Loneliness is one of the most threatening experiences we can have."* Social scientists have concluded that those with strong social networks have built up a strong 'social immune system' that protects their mental and physical health.

Which brings me back to another reason why I love redwood trees. It's because, to me, they represent this 'social immune system' that Steve Cole talks about. Just like redwoods, we humans crave that same sense of connection, belonging and support. A community embraces each other and depends on one another, like an army who has its arms interlocked, standing and strengthening each other. That's why it's so vital for our survival.

All these years later, I do feel connected within a community once again and supported by the people our family has come to know and love. In that season of loneliness though, I had to reach a point where I accepted that no matter what I felt, I knew God was with me and that I was His. I pressed in closer to Him, knowing that not only was He with me, but that ultimately, He is enough in the seasons of lack, loneliness and feeling lost.

I also started to understand, and acknowledge, that developing deep friendships was going to need more than just a few months. Friendships take time. For me, it took recognising other people's needs and reaching out to help them. In turn, and far more difficult, it required letting others help me. When I was able to stop focusing purely on my feelings of loneliness and isolation, and start seeing others' needs around me, I found ways to make connections with them. It was through these experiences that my 'roots' slowly started to interlock and I began to join arms, make friends, build a network and experience 'community' once again.

Reflecting on the connections that were slowly being made in those early years, I realised that they were mostly occurring in the mundane, ordinary moments of the day. When I started to see that these opportunities for bonding and forming attachments could easily be missed if I was not deliberate enough to slow down and to take them, I began to adapt and live differently than I had before.

Life – Altering Encounters

Rewind back to early 2009, in Melbourne, Australia. David and I were sitting on our brand-new leather couch, upon freshly laid floorboards, in our spacious upstairs living area. We'd put our three young children to bed, the youngest just four months old. Unable to have predicted what would happen next, we started watching a DVD. Unaware in that moment, that a simple DVD would be the tool God would use to grip our hearts for something that breaks His: child trafficking. It is moments like this one that we never forget. That moment changed the trajectory of our lives. It demanded that we do something different, something about the 'wrong' that we had become aware of, something to help to make it 'right.' That night, after hearing about ZOE's work in Thailand to help children who had been trafficked, my husband and I looked at each other with tear-stained faces and both knew we had to go.

Our youngest was just one year old when we moved to Thailand. He's a funny little guy. He always had bruised knees and, back then, his mop of blonde curls was always a sweaty mess. He is boisterous, loveable, competitive, funny, loud and outspoken. He's the one who gets away with too much! But he also has a very tender and soft side. A gentle glowing light under his dirt-smeared skin, a sensitive spirit beneath the wrestles, pokes and pranks.

Not so much anymore, but in those first few years, he really could've been half-Thai. From eating fish eyes, frog legs and pig's blood, I'm not sure whether it was the taste that he liked or just the reaction that he got from a welcome audience as he ate them. Although he doesn't eat quite so many exotic foods anymore, he does still love Thai food, oozes energy, loves attention, is loud and rarely sits still.

I always giggle when people say to me, *"Oh it's so great*

that your kids are experiencing such a different way of life. My kids are so ungrateful," or *"Your children must really understand what it's like to go without."* Sorry to say, but my children are children. They struggle with self-centeredness, ungratefulness and not being content just as much as ... well, I do!

I remember one night over dinner; our kids started asking Dave and me, *"Are we rich?"* This led to a long discussion, whereby we turned some questions back to them, *"Do you go to school?" "Do you always have enough to eat?" "Do we have a house to live in?" "Do you know about God?"* The conversation, concluded with us all saying, *"Yes! We are rich!"*

Like other parents I know, I hope for life-changing, 'revelation' moments for my children that rock their world, which challenge their attitudes and inspire them to have a passion that, combined with a love for God, changes lives around them and in turn becomes part of their legacy.

One Sunday night in 2015, we had planned to go to a tourist market to eat from some new food trucks which I had been to with my parents on their recent visit. We were all craving some western food but unexpectedly when we walked there, we found a sign saying that it is closed on Sundays. The problem was that we still had the hankering for a treat, so we decided to keep walking and see what else we could find. Eventually we came to a restaurant where we had been before so we stopped to order some food. With much anticipation we waited and eventually we were served. It did not disappoint! We all enjoyed the special dinner and decided to keep some remaining pizza slices for the next day's lunch as the kids would be at home due to it being school holidays.

By the time we left, it was dark and the footpaths were uneven so we carefully walked single file and held each other tightly as we crossed the busy city roads. It was just as we were about to walk into our street that we saw him ... a man with his t-shirt wrapped over his head and covering his face. He was curled up on the steps of our local church, sleeping, with no home and no bed. It became quickly apparent that our children had also noticed the man as they began to wipe tears from their eyes, but most surprisingly was just how confronted they felt and within seconds, wailing sprung forth from our youngest ... big, gushing tears mixed with ... *"that's just so sad!"*

Without hesitation, we all knew that we had something in our hands ... something we could give. The treat we had earlier thought of saving for ourselves was carefully placed beside the sleeping man and as prayers were tearfully uttered, we walked on. As we rounded the next corner, into our street, we saw yet another man, sleeping in a similar position and rugged up with clothes covering his head. Our little one's sobbing increased. I held his hand. I was taken aback by his reaction but could also see that this must be the first time he had really noticed someone like this or was old enough to understand. "It *is* sad," I agreed. I held his hand tight. The road was dark and quiet save for the noise from his crying.

I searched my heart to find what it was that I really wanted him to know at that moment. I struggled for the words. It was then that my dad's encouragement, spoken out to each of our children on his last day in Thailand came flooding back. He was so right, how he had summed up each of the children.

"That soft and gentle heart that you have, God gave you that heart ... ", I began. *"Remember how Gramps noticed the way that you have names for all your soft toys and the way you care for them? And the way you tenderly treat animals? That sadness that you feel when something is not right ... God must feel like that too. But He is going to use that softness in you so that you can help people. Don't ever forget what you saw tonight. When it makes you feel sad, you can use that to go and make a difference."*

His crying continued into the night. As I lay down next to him and patted him to sleep, I stared down at his little tear-streaked face and remembered back to that night on our new leather couch, all those years ago, when I had wept too for those who do not have a home or a family or know what it really means to be loved.

I choose to share this little story for those of us who are raising children or influencing them as they grow up. Let's continue to pray that the children in our spheres have life-altering moments that begin to shape them and inspire them to be all that they were created to be. And in our own lives, let's continue to open up our eyes to see the needs around us; never forgetting the ones that Jesus made time for during His time on earth — those who don't know yet where hope, love and peace really come from. I'm thankful that this situation allowed us to not only have many more conversations within our family, but also to act upon the needs that we saw that night. I believe that if we continue to let God work through our feelings of sadness, anger and injustice, in combination with His love for people, we will make a difference and really see changes in our circles of influence.

Three years later in church one day, a man named Paul got up to share a testimony. He started by asking us if we had seen the homeless man that slept on the steps at the front of the church. Many of the congregation knew of him. Paul shared that one day the police had come by the church offices and asked him if he had given the homeless man permission to be there. Paul said he hadn't, to which the police officer informed him that he planned to go and command the man to leave. Paul politely asked the police officer if he would allow him one week to find a place for the homeless man to go. The police officer agreed. Through a connection Paul had, a place became available at a home that helps care for people without a support network. They were willing to accept the man, with a week's trial first for good behaviour. The man passed the first week and has continued to live there, supported financially by people who give towards helping to cover his costs. There were so many other testimonies that Paul shared relating to ministry opportunities that had arisen from this home; but what was so wonderful about this story was ... to be reminded about this particular man that our family had all encountered years prior; and to once again be given an opportunity to help him. We discussed how much we wanted to give as a family and how we'd had the privilege of making a small difference in his life.

Idols

When I was a young adult, I spent a few summers on a Scripture Union beach mission team at a place called Tidal River in Wilson's Promontory National Park (aka 'The Prom') in Victoria. It's a really beautiful place and being on a beach mission was an amazing experience. The large team was made up of volunteers from churches across Victoria who desired to serve people camping at The Prom over the summer, and to share the good news that God loves them! The mission at Tidal River had been run every summer for over 50 years. Each year we would get a team t-shirt and I remember this one year our shirt had the verse from Jeremiah 29:13 on the back which read, *'You will seek me and find me when you seek me with all your heart.'*

If you've travelled to Asia, or visited Thailand, you probably noticed that there are many Buddha statues around. Approximately 95 percent of Thailand's population is Buddhist, 300,000 are monks and Thailand is home to more than 40,000 temples (called 'wats'). Honestly, before moving to Thailand, I never really thought too much about idols. I had read about them in Bible stories, but since I didn't grow up surrounded by spirit houses and food offerings, I probably just thought they were a thing of the past. That was until 2012 when I was part of a Bible Study group called 'No Other Gods.'

During that study I learnt many things about how idols are any other 'thing' besides God that we set our heart on, that rule us, that we fear, trust or serve. And I learnt that there were actually modern-day equivalents in my own heart that were competing for God's rightful place in my life. I knew it because I could see that there were things that I craved, desired and thought about more than God. Even though I professed with my mouth that God was number one, I identified that other things were actually operating and functioning as gods in my life, which meant that I couldn't possibly be seeking Him with 'all of my heart.'

I realised that every time I turned to those other things (or other people) for approval, comfort, love or satisfaction; I was inadvertently turning my back on God and not putting Him in His rightful place or living devoted to Him. Whenever I did this, I would feel oppressed by these false gods. My self-worth would fluctuate, I would feel disappointed, I would have unmet expectations, feel insecure or be craving more from these 'idols' than they could ever provide. I had allowed these 'things' to have power over me.

Through the study, I learnt that God in His goodness and love does not want me to live in bondage or like a slave. He wants me to rely on Him. He wants me to seek Him more than anything else. He wants me to give up the things I crave more than Him and in return He'll give me His power to do what I can't do on my own. He was challenging me to surrender to His control. But I had to accept the truth of my own weakness along with accepting the gift of His strength. Recognising that I was powerless on my own brought freedom! And I was one step closer to making room for God to live unrivaled in my heart and living a God-centered life. And that verse in Jeremiah ... I absolutely love this version from the Message Bible, "When you come looking for me, you'll find me. Yes, when you get serious about finding me and want it *more than anything else*, I'll make sure you won't be disappointed."

I Can

For most of the time that we've lived overseas, whatever happens in Thailand or Australia, feels quite separate from each other. But when we departed Thailand to visit Australia in July 2018, I realised that it was not just Thais, but people all over the world, who were mesmerised by news reports updating the progress of rescuing 12 young boys who had gotten lost and stuck in a flooded cave in Chiang Rai. Even in Australia, the story was being followed on every radio and television channel, and it felt like across the globe, thoughts and prayers were focused on bringing those boys out to safety.

During the cave rescue mission, sadness and shock set in when the news came that Petty Officer Saman Gunan, former Thai navy diver, lost consciousness on his way out of the Tham Luang cave and died. He will be forever remembered and honoured for his heroic efforts in the rescue mission.

There were many other heroes too, who the world may not remember or even know their names but who, behind the scenes, did their 'one thing' to help. Rawinmart Luelert is a name you might not recognise. I stumbled upon her story quite by chance. Rawinmart has a factory with 14 washing machines and 15 dryers, and a business which provides laundry services for hotels in her area. When her friend showed her photos of the rescue workers wearing dirty uniforms, she knew there was a way that she could help. Collecting the uniforms of rescue workers every night at 9pm, she gathered a team and worked for ten days straight, returning the uniforms at 4am after cleaning them at her laundry. She shared her appreciation for her employees, volunteers, and friends who helped her work through the night to get the job done. One man, Suwan Kankeaw, who helped to wash the uniforms of the US Navy divers said, "I don't have the ability to get the kids out directly, but what I *can* do is wash these clothes."

As I read about Rawinmart's and Suwan's stories, along with other volunteers who for 12 days prepared 400 boxes of food for lunch and dinner each day ... or who provided foot massages and haircuts for the rescue team ... the stories of these people have stuck in my mind.

At ZOE, not all of us directly rescue children from slavery. There are so many of us working in various teams and departments with a range of tasks, but each of us has an area that we use our skills in to support the work of rescue and make a difference. Just like Suwan, who knew he wasn't the one to get the boys out directly, we can take encouragement from him and so many of the other lesser-known heroes, by discovering what we *can* do — and then make a difference in that space.

I don't know about you, but unfortunately one of the obstacles that has prevented me from helping is when I've focused on what I can't do, or the size of the problem, or I've been afraid of even trying because my efforts might not be as good as I would hope or imagine.

Anyone else have a fear of failure out there? I often feel like the 'me' I want to be doesn't match up with the 'me' I actually am. And what I *want* to achieve and what I actually *do* achieve are two completely different things. The 'me' I want to be has a month of meals pre-planned, an empty ironing basket, cookies baking in the oven, a husband who knows how much he's adored, updated family photos on the wall, waxed legs, children who never argue, friends who feel appreciated, kind words flowing from my lips, a house that looks like something from a 'Pinterest' page, emails replied to ...

I want to be able to look at what I do and say, "*Nailed It!*" You get the picture.

The woman who glances in the mirror, as she rushes off to work often reflects ... *mascara forgotten! Hair needing a wash! Outfit not thoroughly thought through! Hairy legs! Tired eyes!*

Grumpy words and a look of disappointment ... disappointed at the 'image' that she fails to measure up to and frustrated about what she desperately wants to be, but continually seems to fall short of ...!

I catch myself asking, "Is it even possible to be the loving wife, the mother, the friend, the daughter, the sister and the missionary that I strive to be?" But that question leads me to remember — it's not about 'me.' My mission in life is not about trying to 'be' someone or 'do' something that I can never really live up to. When it all boils down, when I reflect on what my Heavenly Father has done for me, all I want is to be the 'me' He wants me to be. And to understand that if I never 'do' another single thing for Him, He still loves me.

All through the Gospels I read passages where Jesus is quoted saying, "Follow Me." When I think about it though, to be a 'follower' of Jesus means I actually have to shadow, or copy, what He did. It sounds so easy, but how hard it can often be. I love how simply John 13: 34 lays it out, "A new command I give you: Love one another. As I have loved you, so you must love one another." And of course, the greatest commandment of all, *"Love the Lord your God with all your heart and with all your soul and with all your mind."* (Matthew 26:37)

As simple as they sound — 'love God' and 'love others' — these words come with a sense of both 'freedom' and 'restriction' at the same time. Or, as Ken Gire explains in his book, 'The Reflective Life,' they feel both 'liberating' and 'confining.' He explains, "Liberating, because it means we are free to do whatever we want. Confining, because it means our love for God sets the boundaries of that freedom. It guides every thought, every action, every conversation. And it does so every minute of the day, every day of our life."

The 'me' I want to be can no longer be measured by how well-groomed or well-organised I am, how 'perfectly' I try to present myself in terms of my domestic abilities or my feeble attempts to appear like I have it all together. If loving God is what's driving my thoughts, actions and conversations then it seems at the end of the day I must ask myself, "Did I love well? Did I reflect love in the busyness of the morning rush to work and school with my husband and children? Did love drive the conversations I had with my friends, and steer each decision I had to make and the reaction given?"

One of my favourite quotes from Mother Teresa is *"If you can't do great things, do little things with great love. If you can't do them with great love, do them with a little love. If you can't do them with a little love, do them anyway. Love grows when people serve."*

I personally think that Jesus is the best model of what a loving, servant heart looks like. And that God is the perfect example of what our character should reflect because of the love, mercy and grace that He first showed us. When I draw near to God and let Him fill my heart with His perfect love, when I love and serve others as Christ did; then I am the 'me' God wants me to be and I no longer need to strive to be anything else because that is enough. I am enough because He is. My identity is complete within Him.

Not Perfect, Still Beautiful

How hard it is to live, remembering that I am enough through Him. Because, I admit it, I do love it when things work out perfectly. Whether it is a cake I'm baking, an event I'm helping to plan, or even a family holiday. Many of my friends know that I have wrestled with fear for years in regard to speaking Thai, but fewer people probably realise that I also struggle speaking English too ... okay, so not one-on-one, or in small groups, but in front of large crowds — I am literally a mess. And I think it's all because I want it to sound perfect and if it's not going to be, then ... (*sigh*). This topic could have a chapter all of its own!

In 2016, our family had an opportunity to take a much-needed getaway with just us five. I was super-excited to have planned the PERFECT trip away. The plan was to have 'no plan.' Just stay at the beach and relax and hang out together. We were all looking forward to some serious family time together. At that stage, we had been living in a transitional home for exactly 12 months. This home had been a stepping stone for the children leaving ZOE because they were graduating high school and beginning university or looking for full-time work. It had been a roller coaster ride of emotions and craziness. It had stretched us in ways that we didn't realise we could be stretched and challenged us tremendously. My heart had broken, once again, for the precious children that ZOE rescues. Our prayers had cried out for the healing transformations needed to bring life back to hearts that ached to feel loved and accepted and longed for moments when these precious young adults would really understand who they are — precious and worthy.

Well, our holiday location was perfect. All the 'bits' that I was able to control and organise worked out really well. But despite the 'perfect' setting, and many wonderful bonding moments and laughter ... our beautiful holiday also included an ugly side of bouts of diarrhea, sunstroke, vomiting, an ear infection and five people who all desperately needed time and space to unwind, process and relax in their own individual ways!!

You get the picture ... ?!

As the holiday drew to a close, and those who had been sick started to feel a bit better, we decided to take one last leisurely stroll along the beach at sunset. A few nights prior, I had found such a really nice large shell. Even some people commented on it as they were passing by. So, on this final night, I had just one more opportunity to scout the beach while the tide was out and I was determined to find another 'perfect' shell for my collection.

My eldest son and I were walking together, eyes both scouring the sand when we began to chat about various things. *"Isn't it amazing,"* I said, *"how we all have such different tastes about what beauty is? Like, I might pick up this shell and think it is so pretty, but you might be thinking it's average and then you see a shell that you really like, and I might not think it's very special at all."* He agreed. Moments later, he produced a shell for me, *"Is this what you're looking for Mum? You can have it!"*

"Aww thanks," I replied. At first glance it looked good but then I noticed something and my perfectionist side dominated, *"But actually I won't keep this one. See, it's broken."*

His next words left me speechless.

"Yes, Mum it is, but even broken shells are beautiful." His words stuck in my mind and began playing over and over. He was so right.

Later that night after finishing a movie we'd started watching the day before, Dave and I were just about to give the instruction for the kids to head off to bed, when my daughter spoke up suggesting we have a time of prayer as a family, thanking God for this wonderful time away that we'd had together. We all agreed ... it was a great idea. I love hearing my children pray. It gives me such insight into their hearts and minds.

After we'd prayed, she suggested that we also have a time of encouragement for one another. Isn't it awesome when you see your children take the lead on the things that you, as the parent, usually instigate? Towards the end of the time, I decided to share the conversation from the beach earlier. I spoke about how it had reminded me that although we still have areas of our lives that are being transformed, God sees us as perfect. We were all broken, but now we can focus on the finished work of Jesus in our lives and know that we are perfect and beautiful to Him. And with the realisation that God sees us and other people, through eyes of love, we too are able to see others in the same way — once broken yet now beautiful!

After we'd talked about this, my daughter came to whisper closely. *"At the start of the week, I used to only collect the perfect shells too, Mum"* she said quietly, *"But then my brother explained to me how when a shell is broken, you can see right inside the shell, which you can't normally see. He said that some shells aren't that nice to look at on the outside but on the inside they're beautiful."* Yet another sweet reminder. God does not look at the things people look at. People look at the outward appearance, but the Lord looks at the heart (I Samuel 16:7).

Our holiday ended faster than I would've liked (why is that?), and it was time to trade wading through warm salty water for the long list of emails and 'to-do' list that awaited me. As I skim read through my inbox, one email jumped off the screen asking would I share with the other missionaries at a meeting that coming week about the Transitional Home that we were living in. Despite the fact that this request made me feel physically sick (did I mention my fear of speaking in public?) and my heart started racing faster than a Japanese bullet train, I was reminded that while I may not ever be a perfect public speaker, what I could share was what God was doing beautifully in, and through the home. The progress in the lives of the young adults who came in and out ... and what God was doing in my own family too.

It can be messy at times to strip away masks and expose inner fears but through God's grace and love we can experience beautiful hope, healing, authenticity and love only made possible because of Him. I was also reminded that if I always operate in my own strength and gifts, I miss out on seeing God show up and be glorified in and through my weakness. Trying to embrace my weaknesses is proving to be one hard task, but when I can see them as opportunities for less of 'me' and more of Him, I am able to break through barriers of fear and take risks allowing Him to be seen working in me more clearly. Isn't it wonderful news that God doesn't need us to try to be perfect? He sees us as perfect already, and He can handle our feelings of brokenness and He makes it into something new — broken — yet beautiful!

Moments in Time

Sometimes it's the very small moments in time that leave the biggest imprints on our lives. Matt Morton, pastor, husband, dad, and author says, *"God is always speaking, in every place and at every moment. He speaks through the world around us. He speaks through his word, and He speaks through the circumstances of our lives, even when our lives seem chaotic or random."*

One day in 2013, I sat marking spelling tests whilst queuing in line for a medical examination that I needed for my work- permit. I had been teaching English to a couple of groups of newly rescued teenagers. Suddenly, I gazed around the room and a large poster hanging on the wall caught my eye. It read, *"You are what you think you are."* It was an advertisement for a local university. But just as quickly as the words sunk in, I caught myself disagreeing with that statement. Not sure about you but, quite honestly ... I am *SO* glad that I am not what I think I am! I reflected back just half an hour prior. How that ten-minute drive to the hospital had seen me on the brink of tears due to anxiety. I had done it again ... the petrol tank was flashing 'empty' and there was no petrol station in sight.

I know, I know, really bad ... I agree!

But I am also so glad that the statement on that poster is not true. What I thought of myself at that moment of neglecting to have enough petrol in my car, does not reflect who I really am. Maybe you don't struggle with forgetfulness like me. Perhaps it's low self-esteem, a challenge with anger or feelings of unworthiness.

Around this same time, I took my son shoe shopping. He'd outgrown his beloved fluorescent yellow soccer shoes and needed something suitable for kicking around in at school. Setting his criteria from the beginning he told me they had to match the school uniform, so we set off to the small selection of shops that sell kid's sizes. I was skeptical about finding anything on the first attempt, but my son is a keen shopper and has a determination to match. He was there to hunt and gather.

After searching around a little bit, we came across a pair of shoes that he really liked. The only issue was that they had laces and, up until this point, because we are always taking our shoes on and off here in Thailand, he hadn't had any need to tie laces yet. I admit I was feeling hesitant. I tried to steer him towards a different pair and talk him out of the laced pair, knowing that it would put pressure on his friends or teacher to be the one doing up the laces 15 times a day! But here's what happened next. As I am ranting and raving and giving all the reasons why laces wouldn't be a good idea, he cuts in "*Mum!*" (in a 'calm down' voice) then he continued, "*But I can do all things through Him who gives me strength.*" I stopped, speechless. "*If that verse is true, then I can learn to tie my shoes and you won't have to help me. I can do it. I can learn!*"

I love it when my kids remind me of things that I should already 'know.' I love it when the truth planted in a little heart every day over eight years, springs to life; when seeds sown begin to sprout. In that moment ... he knew where to find the truth. Even as mothers, we can temporarily lose sight of who our children really are. I'm glad God doesn't!

We have a couple of statements in our house for when someone does or says something unkind. We say, "That's not like you" or "That's not who you are."

When the world around you is bombarding you with messages telling you that you must look a certain way to be acceptable, be a particular size or have this type of phone/car/house ... whatever it is, who will you listen to? Are you who you think you are? Are you who others think you are? I believe we should know the truth. Let go of who you think you are and trust that you are who God says you are. When wrong thoughts come, don't spend time entertaining them. Let God's truth dominate your mind!

Another time, in 2013, I was doing some relief teaching at the school where my children attended. This particular morning, while I was helping cut rambutans for fruit-break, I accidentally slipped with the knife and sliced the top of my finger. As blood spurted out, I wrapped my other hand around it and made my way to the staff area to wash it off and survey the damage. Next, I started searching for the rather large, Band-Aid supply (crucial in any school) and located it in the cupboard of the preschool teacher's room. As my first-aid action began, a conversation started with one of the other teachers who happened to be in the office working at the time — a conversation that most likely would not have occurred had it not been for the slip of that knife.

In the context of ordinary life, I marvel at the gift of 'moments in time' when a precious conversation occurs right there amongst the busyness of the day, amid the blood, the Band-Aid wrappers and the lesson preparations. That conversation, on a regular school day, was the beginning of a much deeper friendship over the next few years. I am so thankful for the opportunities I have to be a part of the ups and downs of people's lives and them mine, to stand with them in prayer, believe with them in faith and for these unplanned 'moments' (however painful they may begin) that lead us to stop ... talk ... and share.

When we uprooted our family from our comfortable life in Melbourne, we surrendered 'our plans' and began a new journey having experiences that we never could have imagined, or coped with, on our own. God has faithfully proven that He is with us, every step of the way. I am repeatedly being challenged to learn to trust Him and lean not on my own understanding, no matter what struggles I find myself, or my family in. In those early years, I was beginning to learn that I had a choice to allow God to work in the midst of it all or try to manage on my own. He was always there with me, but it took me training my eyes to see, my ears to hear, and my heart to receive what He was doing in each and every moment.

It makes me sad to think about it, but I know for sure there have been so many times when I have missed knowing and being part of people's lives, because I walked right by without making any connection. Sometimes I blame being an introvert, or being too busy or being distracted, but it continues to be true that in the moments when I have allowed myself to pause and be impacted by the details of the lives around me; I get to see people's value and worth. It shifts my focus off my own goals and desires and on to the realisation that it is in these moments that God is working in their lives, through me, and in mine, through them. I want to look forward, with joyful expectation, to the unplanned moments in each new day. Choosing to honour the interruptions and not see them as an inconvenience, or ruining my plans, but simply as gifts. I am learning that these unexpected experiences in life impact me, and those around me, in life-giving ways. When I pass them by, I lose the opportunity to touch other's lives and for them to touch mine like the redwood, and their intertwined roots.

Full of Life

The Christmas season in Thailand is so completely different for me in comparison to the traditions that I grew up with in Australia. December comes, and I compare in my mind how there's no junk mail filled with tempting gift ideas shoved into the mailbox. We don't watch television — so there are no advertisements proclaiming the newest 'thing' that we need.

Back in 2010 when we arrived in Thailand, besides some random attempts by the big department stores to pretty things up with lights and a few artificial trees, there were not too many other clues that Christmas was just around the corner.

One year when I was taking down the tree, I felt particularly reflective. I was remembering all the fun we used to have in Australia going to the Christmas tree farm and choosing a real tree and chopping it down. How every year it looked different and smelled so good ... ooh that smell of pine needles. I do miss that smell. I also reminisced as I carefully took each decoration off and placed them on the couch. I thought about how, before we had children, our tree was all perfectly colour-coordinated. How we had bought some really special decorations when we were first married but now, after so many Christmases, they looked very ... worn.

I noticed the decorations we made at ZOE one year, and I gazed at the star and the tinsel that our friends had sent us in the mail for our first Christmas in Thailand. I admired the beautiful angel ornament a friend just gave me in support of the Kachin people in Burma, the star made by a young lady with HIV which we bought at church, the little grass nest which holds a bird, woven by a little girl at ZOE and given to my daughter ... and, of course, all the wonderful decorations that our three children had made at school over the years when their chubby little fingers were still learning to cut and colour-in. These are what make our tree so imperfect that it is so perfect! In all its scrawniness and plasticity, I admit, I love it that now our tree is so full of 'life' — not in the sense of being a real tree, but as a reflection of the life we have as a family, who we are and the memories we've made together.

The true meaning of Christmas, and what Jesus' birth means to us, prompts me to think about the life we have and His most important gift of all.

Around the time of my children's birthdays, I also remember back to the times surrounding their impending arrivals and take a few moments to reflect on the events that surrounded each of their births.

I was recently reminded of when I went into labour with my first son and the unexpected occurred ... I needed an emergency C-section! The medical staff spun into action around me, making the journey from delivery room to surgery fast. Rushing is necessary sometimes! And similarly, around the season of Christmas, I remember not only our Saviour's birth, but I am again reminded of the events leading up to it.

As Mary rode uncomfortably on the donkey's back, there must have been a sense of urgency to get to Bethlehem as quickly as possible. I imagine, upon arrival, the climate intensified as they kept being turned away, searching for a place to stay.

"There's no room here," yet another innkeeper replied.

"Please hurry Joseph!" Mary's eyes pleaded in panic.

"I'm trying Mary! ... " Joseph quietly soothed, desperately racing to knock on the next closed door. "We need a room quickly."

Reflecting on my own life, I can identify with those 'rushing' moments of medical emergencies, racing through airports to make connecting flights, border-runs, visas needing urgent approval, Christmas shopping ... and the list goes on.

But Mary treasured up all these things and pondered them in her heart. (Luke 2:19 NIV)

Despite the urgency of Mary's situation, we read that she

had this beautiful way of treasuring things in her heart, of remembering, and thinking about them deeply. Through the unexpected twists and turns of her life, Mary slowed down enough to pause ... to think and to consider.

Maybe her mind couldn't fully make sense of all God had planned, but instead of doubting what He was doing, she remained full of faith, trusting God through the 'unknowns' that lay before her. And so, at Christmas time, I remind myself again to stop rushing about and to simply treasure in my heart the most amazing, generous, miraculous gift of Jesus. The blessings of peace, the beauty of hope, the spirit of love, the comfort of faith. These are His gifts to us.

Whether you usually have a white Christmas or a scorching hot one, a real pine tree or small plastic one like ours, I hope that you find peace and joy knowing that Jesus came to this Earth for you. His life is a gift for each of us to accept. The sacrifice of His death means that we can have life and have it to the full — forever.

When the decorations are put away for another year, and the tree folded down once more, so begins a new season. With so many goals and dreams for the year ahead, I am reminded again in this season to cast aside my doubts and uncertainty, choosing to remain full of faith and trust in God through the unknowns in life.

Mystery Customer

At the beginning of 2020, I was asked to share a devotion with the kitchen staff at ZOE in their department meeting. This group of people are equally as amazing as the staff who help rescue children and yet many times, their work goes unnoticed. As I was praying about what to share, I felt like God was asking me to talk about an experience I'd had working in a restaurant in my teenage years.

You've probably heard statistics that say 90% of customers who have an unhappy experience at a restaurant won't say anything directly, but basically they'll just go somewhere else. There's a quote: "*If you have a good experience in a restaurant, you'll tell two people. If you have a bad experience, you'll tell ten people.*"

When I worked in a restaurant, our manager was acutely aware of these statistics and would spend a great deal of time telling us to 'keep cleaning' and reminding us of many other things that we had to do. It became a bit like white noise because it happened so often but every once in a while, we would understand why he was saying it because we would have a "mystery customer" come to our restaurant. A mystery customer looks like a normal diner, but they are there to write a report and submit details and feedback about their experiences while eating at the restaurant. Sometimes one of the restaurant staff would guess there was a mystery customer and, as word spread, we would all be conscious about being friendly and keeping everything clean, etc. But most times we didn't know who it was or when they'd come until afterwards. Later on, we would find out how they rated us ... but at the time we didn't realise we were being watched carefully.

So, with the ZOE kitchen staff, I had brought in two plates of sliced apples to the meeting. They both looked the same. But I asked them, "If I told you that one of these plates of food was prepared by someone who chopped the apple on the floor and one who used the bench, could you tell?" Then I continued, "If I said one of these plates was prepared by someone who went to the bathroom and didn't wash their hands properly, could you tell?" Or "What if I said that someone blew their nose and then touched the food? Which one would you want to eat?" But "We can't tell right?" And then I asked, "So why does it matter if we do or don't do those things, if no-one can tell?

I am a qualified teacher. As part of working in a school, I knew that my principal would walk around checking in on teachers. I knew I'd have to write reports, meet with the parents and have work samples up on the wall so parents could see what I was teaching and for accountability. Next, I shared about how, when we moved to Thailand, I was praying "Lord show me what area at ZOE 1 will work in" but at a women's conference God told me that in that season, my ministry was at home.

Being at home alone, if I didn't look after my small children, who would've even known? What if I yelled at them? What if I didn't give them toys to play with or just sat them in front of the television all day? What if I didn't do a good job? Who would've seen? I decided back then that even if I didn't have a job that people could see, I would do my job the best I could. Even though no one knew, I would cook healthy food. I would train myself to be patient and talk to my children respectfully. I would play with them and read to them even though no one else knew or could see what I did. I would keep the house tidy and mop the floor (often). Who else knows that having small children is messy? But I decided that I would mop that floor to the glory of God. Even when no one else could see, even though no one else was walking around checking my work or giving me a report or even telling me 'good job,' I chose to do a good job.

Colossians 3 verses 23-24 say, "*Whatever you do, work at it with all your heart, as working for the Lord, not for people, since you know that you will receive an inheritance from the Lord as a reward. It is the Lord Christ you are serving.*" NIV

And just like I wanted to encourage the kitchen staff who probably don't get as much praise or acknowledgment as they deserve, I want to encourage you, too. Whatever you're asked to do, whether you think "it doesn't matter," "no one will know," "anyone could do this" ... work as if you're working for the Lord. Maybe no one can tell — just like the plates of sliced apple. But ask yourself, would you want to eat the one with germs all over it? Would it be good enough to serve Jesus if He walked into the room?

You might not be thanked very often. People might complain or not appreciate all that you do but you're not working for them, you're working for the Lord. He deserves more than any mystery customer! He deserves our very best. If no one else sees, He sees.

New Year

Flashback to January 1st, 2018, and I looked around to see our house in a crazy state of mess. There was a tent drying in the lounge room and sleeping bags scattered all over the floor, an ice box in the passageway and backpacks leaning against the tubs of packed (but not yet put away) Christmas decorations. The washing machine was on and camping mats were creating an obstacle course around the first-aid kit and the leftover snacks! But this 'mess' represented an unforgettable two days away camping that even the most disorderly house could not take away.

The three exhausted children, who the night before had squealed, ran, hid and played hard for hours in the dark, now slept peacefully. As they toasted marshmallows and shared their memories from the year just past and their hopes and dreams for the one ahead, I was reminded how blessed I was to be their mother. I reflected on the night, sitting around the mesmerising campfire, listening to them giggle and chatter and reminisce — all the while making the last few, lasting memories in the final hours of 2017.

It had been an interesting year. The five of us each chose one word to describe it. 'Unexpected,' 'Jam-packed,' 'Trust,'

'Challenging' and then our youngest, who couldn't narrow it down to just one word, came up with 'Fard' (Fun+ Hard)!

I had laughed as my kids re-enacted my most embarrassing moments, but also listened in amazement when one of them shared a really embarrassing thing that had happened to them, being vulnerable, open and honest. When I stop dwelling on all the areas that they need improvement in and I see glimpses of the growth they've experienced this past year, I am so thankful.

The made-up word 'fard' did sum up the previous year quite well. There were incredibly fun moments and there were tremendously hard ones too but through all the challenges and unexpected twists and turns, we definitely all grew in our trust in God.

I read an email shortly after entitled 'What is My One Word?' It was this quote though, in the email, that caught my eye and spoke straight to my heart. PAUSE. My word for the year is PAUSE. In my busy life there are so many times I need to pause. Pause to remember these days, for they will fly by so quickly. Pause to say yes ... and no. Pause to give thanks. Pause before I speak in anger, judgment, or criticism. Pause to say I'm sorry. Pause to dwell on God's goodness and mercy.

And so, as I headed into another new year, I chose to focus on the growth — developed in trusting God and leave behind the disappointments, failures and unmet expectations. I reminded myself (once again) to embrace hope, joy and love. And to make a decision ... to PAUSE more in the year ahead ... slow down and be thankful.

In that same week a friend sent me a message that said, "I was touched by the Emmanuel song at church — God coming down to be with us in our messy lives ... "

How lovely to be reminded that He is with us in the 'fun+hard' times.

Summer Drought

In 2016, we experienced an even hotter summer than usual with one of the warmest years in Thailand; and one of the hottest days on record since 1955, and, although April in Thailand is typically hot, there was also a new record set for the longest heat wave in at least 65 years. I remember weeks and weeks of temperatures hovering around 40 degrees and above.

In the year leading up to our departure to Thailand, I felt closer to God than I ever had before. I had sought Him and heard from Him clearly leading up to our 'scout trip' to Thailand and I knew that my heart was being prepared for what was ahead of us.

When we booked tickets to see ZOE for the first time, we sensed something was happening by the resistance that we got when trying to organise our trip. I'll never forget the night we needed to book our flights ... from our passports strangely disappearing, our young baby screaming uncontrollably (which was totally out of character), the internet kept disconnecting and then David's crown on his front tooth completely fell out!

If we had a single doubt about God calling us to ZOE in our minds before going to see, we certainly did not arrive home from our scout trip with any. We were blown away with how much God had gone before us. He gave us a week full of confirmations from particular songs being played, Bible verses spoken to us, and people saying things in conversations that spoke straight to our hearts. God completely showered us with His love and He showed us that He is the God of detail. He loves to pay attention to the little things that matter to us. We had an amazing week and met some of the most precious people. Their hearts and their passion were incredibly impactful. It was just so inspiring to be around.

There have been seasons in my life where I have felt fully alive. This was one such time. It was like God was literally right there with me. Summer has a wonderful way of capturing beauty, the glistening sunshine on the water, the bright colours of nature and the magical warm nights that mean you can stay outdoors just a little bit longer than normal.

During the season of summer though, there can also be times of extreme drought. Right before your eyes, the same front lawn that you literally just frolicked on bare-foot, under the sprinkler weeks earlier has now turned brittle and brown, scratching the soles of your feet. The flowers that a few days prior had been out in vibrant bloom, now appear wilted and dying in the scorching heat. As the dust settles, and an unquenchable thirst tempts us to turn to anything that will satisfy, it's the beginning of the wilderness and wanderings — when will it rain again?

When we so urgently want something, or someone, to bring us relief in these times of drought, it's hard not to just 'fill' the void with whomever, or whatever we think will refresh us and bring the quickest relief. Unfortunately, in the past, I have done this. Looked to friends, family, material possessions or my achievements to fill my emptiness instead of drawing closer to the real source of the refreshment that I so desperately need — and depending on God for survival. It was only when I understood that God actually *wants* to meet me in these dry, desert places, that I see the desert as the very place where He speaks and calls me back to Himself.

Characterised as a Type Seven on the Enneagram, I can see in myself the tendency to avoid pain. So, I think I have tried to avoid the desert experiences, or at least I saw them as a negative place to be. Recently though, I learned that the Hebrew word for 'desert' is *'midbaar'* meaning 'to speak.' This redefines the desert for me. Now I see it is actually a place to hear God's voice. This gives me confidence that whatever 'desert' I go through God will have something to say to me. I don't need to beg God to get me out of the desert but ask Him what He is teaching me *in* it? And I know I can experience joy and hope even if grief and pain are present.

The danger of remaining in a state of drought is the picture of what life is like without God. Realising that I cannot live without His presence in my life has been an opportunity for spiritual renewal and refreshment. Taking time to reflect on the periods of drought have indeed become sacred parts of my journey. Sometimes the banks burst and the floodgates only open when, on my knees, I have cried out for relief to the only one who can truly give it. It is then that I have fully understood that not one single day of the summer, the desert or the wanderings in the wilderness were wasted. When it seems as though nothing is happening, I will not be discouraged. I believe God uses this season, the summer, to draw us back into His arms.

After more than a decade in Thailand, I know what it feels like to be hot and thirsty. So, echoing the theme found in Psalm 42, I wrote the following response in a ZOE staff meeting one day.

Why Am I Thirsty?

How long could I last without water
In this hot weather?
How long 'til my mouth and throat ... so parched
That I would no longer be able to even utter a word?
Without even a single drop? One day ... three days?
Not long ... at all!
And yet when my soul is dry and parched, panting and longing for a
drink from You God, I often just ignore it.
Why do I neglect my soul?

Why do I allow my spirit to dry up?
I need to drink from You, oh God.
All day. Every day.
Overwhelm me so that I thirst for more and more of You.
The deepest needs in me
Cry out to the even deeper kindness and generosity of Your love.
When I drink You ...
Your waterfall of loving kindness cascades down.
Waves sweep over me and carry me away.
Soaking me abundantly.
Your promises of love pour out over me.
I never need to feel thirsty.
I must drink deeply. For You are enough.

Sept 18th, 2019

Discussion Questions

What impact have the 'summers' of your life had on you? What have they taught you about yourself, your life and others?

Could you relate to the comparison of the redwood trees and living in community? Have you experienced a time of loneliness or isolation that resulted in you needing to rebuild your support network and find new people to connect with?

How can you practically honour the interruptions and the 'unplanned moments' during your day and not see them as an inconvenience, but instead as gifts? Can you think of a time when an unexpected experience impacted you in a life-giving way?

Can you think of a time when embracing weaknesses, or inner fear, you experienced God's strength working in, and through you?

As the world bombards you with messages that you must look a certain way to be acceptable, achieve certain goals or have the right type of phone/car/house. How can you focus on the right messages? What are some practical ways that you can let go of other's opinions of you and your opinion of yourself, to believe that you are who God says you are?

When it seems as though nothing is happening, we must not be discouraged. God uses this season, the summer, to draw us back into His arms. Use the space to write any additional thoughts, verses, encouragements or reflections about summer here:

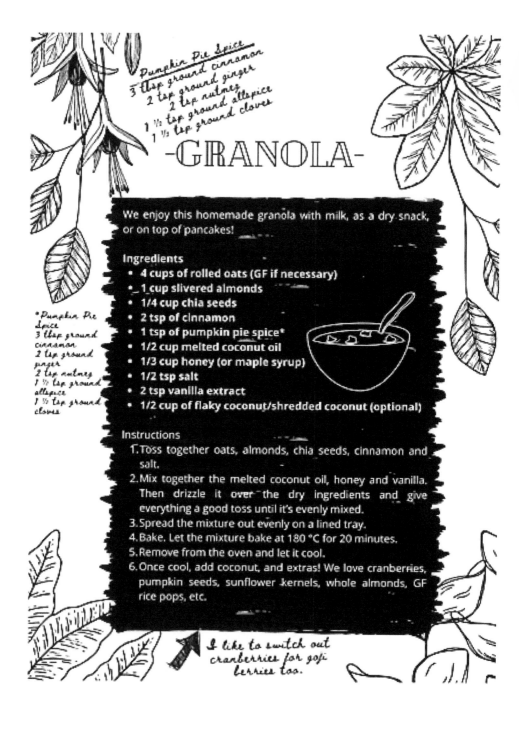

Pumpkin Pie Spice
3 tbsp ground cinnamon
2 tsp ground ginger
2 tsp nutmeg
1 ½ tsp ground allspice
1 ½ tsp ground cloves

-GRANOLA-

We enjoy this homemade granola with milk, as a dry snack, or on top of pancakes!

*Pumpkin Pie Spice
3 tbsp ground cinnamon
2 tsp ground ginger
2 tsp nutmeg
1 ½ tsp ground allspice
1 ½ tsp ground cloves

Ingredients
- **4 cups of rolled oats (GF if necessary)**
- **1 cup slivered almonds**
- **1/4 cup chia seeds**
- **2 tsp of cinnamon**
- **1 tsp of pumpkin pie spice***
- **1/2 cup melted coconut oil**
- **1/3 cup honey (or maple syrup)**
- **1/2 tsp salt**
- **2 tsp vanilla extract**
- **1/2 cup of flaky coconut/shredded coconut (optional)**

Instructions
1. Toss together oats, almonds, chia seeds, cinnamon and salt.
2. Mix together the melted coconut oil, honey and vanilla. Then drizzle it over the dry ingredients and give everything a good toss until it's evenly mixed.
3. Spread the mixture out evenly on a lined tray.
4. Bake. Let the mixture bake at 180 °C for 20 minutes.
5. Remove from the oven and let it cool.
6. Once cool, add coconut, and extras! We love cranberries, pumpkin seeds, sunflower kernels, whole almonds, GF rice pops, etc.

I like to switch out cranberries for goji berries too.

Puts you in a good mood :)

-MOODY SMOOTHIE-

On summer days my husband and I like to make ourselves this Moody Smoothie full of amazing ingredients. I named it Moody Smoothie because one of the ingredients is called "ashwagandha." You can read more about it online but basically is an adaptogenic herb (helps to balance, restore and protect the body). It's valued for its thyroid modulating, neuroprotective, anti-anxiety, antidepressant and anti-inflammatory properties - helping to put you in a great mood.

Ingredients (for 2 people)

- 500ml almond milk
- 2 bananas
- handful of blueberries
- spinach
- 1 tbsp chia seeds
- 2-3 tsp cacao
- 1-2 tsp ashwagandha
- 1 tbsp honey (optional)

And don't opt out on the spinach either, it's high in vitamin D and folate, decreasing negative moods, clinical depression and foggy thinking!

Ashwagandha is a powerful herb that has shown incredible results for lowering cortisol levels and balancing thyroid hormones.

Hello Autumn

'God uses this season to remind us that He is our source of power and strength.'

It had been such a long time since I had experienced any autumn weather, but as my feet crunched down on the large brown leaves which had fallen from the trees on our hike through the bushland, I was momentarily taken back to a place where fiery, earthy colours transformed trees and crisp morning breezes replaced the depth of the hot summer's days. I'd recently had a conversation with my kids when they asked me what autumn was.

"This is what it's like," I yelled to my children walking up ahead armed with a large stick in one hand and a piece of fruit in the other. "These leaves are a little bit like the autumn leaves you'd see in Australia," I added. Or were they? It had been over eight years at that stage since I'd felt an autumn day. When I thought back to the physical attributes of autumn time, growing up in Australia, I remembered the noticeable changes in the landscape and in nature, especially the colour palette. But was stomping through big, crunchy orange and brown leaves and the weather cooling down to a more-comfortable temperature, all there really was to this season? I struggled to recall.

Australia's seasons are at opposite times of the year to those in the northern hemisphere which means that our autumn is March, April and May. When Europeans arrived in Australia, they set new dates for the seasons and chose a more convenient setting, still used by the Bureau of Meteorology today, and based on the first of the month.

I grew up in Melbourne where The Moomba Festival is a big highlight in March. It occurs every year over the Labour

Day weekend and is a four-day event which millions attend. The festival includes live music, carnival rides, lots of food and nightly fireworks. Set on the banks of the Yarra River, world-class water sport athletes from many countries compete in the Moomba Masters Championship; and there's also a Birdman Rally (people showcasing their inventive homemade flying devices). The festival has been held annually in Melbourne since 1954. 'Moomba' is an Australian Aboriginal word meaning 'Let's get together and have fun.' The festival also features a parade that weaves through city streets and is attended by thousands of families. The colourful parade is made up of dance groups, performers, music bands and huge floats. I remember one year when I was about 12 years old, I represented my athletics club in the parade alongside many other community groups.

Autumn is defined as 'the transition months' between the hottest and the coldest times of the year. In the southern states of Australia, autumn represents the anticipation of coming rains, cooler temperatures and a recovery period after a dry, hot summer. Autumn brings a sense of balance — an equinox (a word I struggle to pronounce ... ee·kwuh·nox) which occurs around the 20th -21st -22nd March — bringing an equal length of day and night.

Metaphorically speaking, when I think about the 'autumn' experiences in my life, the positive ones include transition as well as strengthening, maturing, resilience, contentment, embracing change, gaining greater perspective, preparation for winter and facing challenges head-on. The temporary setbacks in this season have been feeling overwhelmed, painful adjustments or creating necessary boundaries.

So, let's begin creating some cozy indoor spaces, having 'Moomba' moments, searching for answers, weighing up options and preparing to let go. Autumn is about accepting that some good things come to an end. This chapter will look at some of the 'autumn' experiences that have taught me so much and given me greater perspective as I have transitioned from summer and prepared for winter.

Where's Thailand?

Growing up, I never imagined living in Thailand, but in January 2010, at 33 years old and with three young children, that is where my husband and I headed. In 2009 we heard about ZOE International and within a year, we had packed up our home in the suburbs of Melbourne and relocated our family to a completely different part of the world to begin a new life working as volunteers fighting child trafficking.

Looking back, we arrived at the Chiang Mai airport with a lot of baggage! In addition to our suitcases, we were also carrying some 'weighty' emotions that came as a result of just having separated ourselves from all that was familiar to us: a life we 'knew', a great family and friendships that had taken decades to develop. It was these 'heavy' thoughts that weighed on me as I looked at my three small children's tear-streaked faces, noticing just how much their contrasting appearances stood out amongst the Thai people. *Would* everything be okay?

I remember how it took every muscle in my body to lift our heavy luggage, but that was nothing in comparison to the 'inner' strength that I needed to help get our family to where we are now. I give all the thanks to God for that strength. I personally could not have survived a month if it had not been for His comfort and peace. We have all wept many tears, we have felt so far away and we have missed our friends and family like crazy. God is so good though and He is faithful. He has blessed us with friends and a community here that I could only dream of when we arrived. These people have loved us through sickness, injuries and burnout. They have laughed and cried with us and they have fiercely stood by us when we were down and given us space when it was needed. It takes my breath away to reflect and see how rich our lives are through having come here and I am so thankful.

During a Geography class back in eighth grade, my teacher had to, once again, separate my friend and me for talking too much. I had a terrible case of 'the giggles' as I reluctantly moved seats to relocate away from my friend. My teacher sternly rebuked my behavior in front of the class and shot me a disapproving look, which meant I needed to get a grip quickly. I tried to refocus by looking down at the atlas that was opened in front of me. We were meant to be committing the countries that belonged in each continent to memory, but to me it was just a blur of coloured, irregular shapes and unusual names — most of them much too difficult for me to memorise. It was not until much later, towards the end of high school that my curiosity and sense of adventure started to increase, leading me to seriously start searching the atlas with a new interest; seeking out places that I'd like to travel to and explore ... Thailand being just one of them!

From the time we were married, Dave and I had a joint passion for helping children. After attending an information session about foster care, we were told that we could apply to become foster parents after being married for one year. So that's what we did. As soon as they approved our application, we spent our time as foster parents as well as buddies on 'Life Gets Better Camps' for children who had gone through major grief (such as divorce or a death in their immediate family). These voluntary roles were fitted in, and around, our family schedule and careers. When we began volunteering, I was a primary school teacher and David was in business.

What impacted us significantly in the season before we moved, was discovering that ZOE was an international Christian organisation that rescued children who were sold, or at risk of being sold, into slavery. They had an aftercare home in Thailand and were caring for precious children, who had been orphaned or were victims of heinous crimes and abuse. The organisation, while raising global awareness about the growing human trafficking epidemic, is dedicated to placing children in families as well as giving hope and a future to those rescued. Over the years ZOE has expanded and (at this writing) is also at work in America, Australia, Japan and Mexico.

When we first heard the statistics about children — not much older than our own — being trafficked, my husband and I felt both overwhelmed and compelled to act. Now, when we see the beautiful faces of the kids at ZOE, each of those 'statistics' are not numbers anymore but precious lives — each on a journey of restoration.

Since moving to Thailand, it has been impossible not to fall in love with the extended ZOE family. The kids, in spite of what they have been through, have amazing testimonies of God's faithful restoration, and the Thai staff and ZOE parents are the most gentle, kind-hearted people that I have ever met. Their attitudes and the way they conduct themselves is remarkable, beyond what I had ever seen or encountered before coming to Thailand. They are so welcoming, appreciative and friendly, but most importantly, they are a family that really knows how to love ... unconditionally!

Adjustment

Moving to Thailand and changing pretty much everything was not easy. It's not only that the lifestyle is so different. It's not just the food, the language or the weather, but the degree of cultural change and adjustment takes a *really* long time and requires a lot of perspective, and patience to even begin to understand.

One adjustment, living as a foreigner, has been the

transient community and way-of-life that we find ourselves thrown into. For our family, just when we made a friend, grew to love a particular teacher, or found a person that we really admired; it seemed they would go ... just like that! And June is still the worst month of all for saying goodbyes. There is a constant stream of new people coming and a constant stream of friends going. Our children have had to say goodbye to countless friends over the years who have gone back to their home countries, moved to a different province or been relocated for their parent's work.

I remember listening to a school counsellor once who was explaining how every time he moved to a different international school, students always ask one question early in the opening conversation and that was, "How long are you here for?" I can see now after having lived overseas for a while, how thoughts like: *"I'm not going to trust you ... spend time with you ... invest in you or let you into my life ..."* can easily arise. When defenses go up and worries creep in that this 'friend' might only share life temporarily, I'll be honest, it's hard to love and open your heart time and time again to people when you know they won't be around for very long. And therein lies one of the biggest challenges of living in a transient community.

I read once:

> *'We're expert farewellers but with every goodbye there is an ignored reality that we don't dare mention out loud. We cover it up with overly optimistic and misguided statements like, "We'll come visit you., and "We'll skype every week." Those well wishes help us feel a little better but they don't come true. The sad truth is that when we say goodbye (with a few beautiful exceptions) we will never see these people again.'*

(Taken from 'Why Expats Hate June')

Many years back, in a season of loneliness, I prayed for some more friends. I have a lot of friends in Australia — really, really good ones but those friendships took years to develop. Some of my closest friends I have known since primary school, so it didn't take me long to figure out that you don't just 'make' friends like *that* overnight.

Back in August 2011 just as one lovely friend Jessica was heading back to America for two months, God sent me another friend. Right in my hour of need, in walked Kaylee all fresh-faced and bubbly from sunny California and I was so thankful when we instantly got along. There was just one catch ... she was only staying for one year!

It would have been easy to keep her at arm's length, to protect my heart. But instead I chose ...

To embrace her.

To be grateful.

To laugh.

To share.

To open up.

To risk the heartache of saying 'see you later,' not ever knowing if, or when, 'later' would ever be. And selfishly when the time came, I didn't want to let her go.

I knew that she was listening to God though, just like she had done when she had packed up and left the comfort of home to come to Thailand. At the end of it all, I was so grateful that she opened up her heart and her life to me. I felt privileged to have met her and, oh, so very grateful for the richness of her friendship over that 12-month period.

I'll never forget when she came to keep me company while Dave was staying in a village several hours away and our conversations at 3 am quickly turned to muffled screams as we tried to fend off the biggest cockroaches, we'd both ever seen. I'll never forget how she became my 6 am walking partner for many months protecting me from stray dogs with her pepper spray on a keychain. I'll never forget when she taught me how to make chai yen (Thai cold tea) and spoilt our family with her delectable, homemade chocolate chip cookies. We shared a love of coffee, shopping and planning parties and we went to Bible study together at the local cafe. After a trip to Bangkok where we visited my friends who lived in a slum, many in-depth discussions took place as we wrestled with our emotional reactions to what we'd seen. And then there was swimming, bowling, teaching English together, the driving lessons, pedicures, eating rotis, sharing Thanksgiving recipes and the funny times we had out and about in Chiang Mai getting lost and mostly just sharing a lot of laughs! I'll always remember Kaylee's love of flowers, glitter, bling, dressing up, painting her nails and all things sparkly. It was so great to have someone like that in my life. It was worth it just to have such a fun friend for a year and definitely an answer to my prayer at that time.

So, the longer I'm here, the more I begin to understand that I have to alter the way I view how life was 'meant to be.' I'm learning that life doesn't follow a 'rule book' and that I'm not 'in control.' *God is!* Regarding transition, the temptation is to stop engaging new people when they come because the pain of saying goodbye (again) is just too much. Even though our natural response to people coming and going is to try to protect our hearts from being hurt. As a parent, what I want to instill in my kids is that, despite the pain of saying goodbye, the greater suffering is to never have allowed ourselves to love. Sometimes I need to think of 'dealing with change' in the words of Winnie The Pooh who said, "How lucky I am to have something that makes saying goodbye so hard."

Deeply Rooted

Whenever I think about the word 'zoe,' images of trees come to mind. In the Bible, the Greek word zoe (ζωή) refers to eternal life with God but, in fact, it changes our earthly lives in every good way too and is offered free for all who believe and accept Jesus.

In many cultures, trees represent life and prosperity. More than 36 different trees are mentioned throughout the Old and New Testaments of the Bible. And let's not forget that Jesus Christ's death on a cross (made from a tree) means that we can have eternal life.

"In many ways, trees are like Jesus. They give, and they keep giving. They give life and beauty. They give shade and rest. They clean the air. They hold back erosion. They offer shelter, food, and protection." (christianity.com)

Most people who know about ZOE are aware of the trafficking side of the work. But as a Christian organisation, we are also passionate about everyone receiving the opportunity to have abundant life with God. We reach out to people who do not yet know about God's love, or the gift of eternal life. Oftentimes this looks like bringing practical help, meeting physical needs and sharing God's plan with people in remote, small, vulnerable and unreached places. But actually, we want our lives to always be reflecting the love of God wherever we are. When we see children experience freedom and healing, it brings us so much joy, but when we see people choose to receive God's 'zoe-life,' we know that they will experience freedom and life forever!

Once I hit my thirties, I stopped thinking about 'growing up' and started to understand the importance of 'growing down' and desired to be deeply rooted in God. Knowing that there is no limit to growing down, but that I can keep discovering more and more about God is so refreshing. The fact that by growing down, I actually become stronger to grow up is just such good news to me, and it alleviates a lot of stress on my part.

What if I really understood that His divine power gives me everything I need to fulfill what He's asked me to do? What if I could grasp that the same power that raised Jesus from the dead lives in me? If I could learn to fully rely on, and be strengthened by Him daily, instead of trying to live by my own efforts, my life would reflect His peace, joy and love ... all the time! I can already see that if my day begins by quieting my heart and directing my thoughts towards God (before I encounter anyone else) it is not only a lot less exhausting but He also empowers me. I love The Passion version of 2 Corinthians 12:9 where the Lord says to Paul, *"My grace is always more than enough for you, and my power finds its full expression through your weakness"* to which Paul's responds, *"So I will celebrate my weaknesses, for when I'm weak I sense more deeply the mighty power of Christ living in me."*

There's a Chinese proverb that says, *"When the roots are deep, there is no reason to fear the wind."* In 2017, while on holidays at the beach, God spoke to my heart using images of 'trees' again. One kind He used was the palm tree. I have a sister-in-law whose name is Tamara, which actually means palm tree, and strength. Palm trees are both beautiful and fruitful. In our home we rely on their fruitfulness for dates in our cooking as well as for coconut oil, but what I really love most about palm trees is their strength.

Our holiday in the south of Thailand was during monsoon season so we experienced heavy rains, lots of wind and big storms while we were there. At night, in our little room on the beach, we could hear the crashing waves and the loud noise of the winds whipping around our surroundings. Heavy rain pounded the roof and each morning as our family exited the room to go to breakfast, I expected to see trees fallen over and damage all around. I was amazed to see just how strong the palm trees were though. There they stood standing tall seemingly unaffected by the storms.

I later found out that in a hurricane, a palm tree can bend all the way to the point where it looks like it's about to break, but it doesn't. That is how God made them. During the storm it's rough and it's harsh on the trees, but after the storm, scientists have proven that palm trees actually become stronger than what they were before.

We live in a world where so many storms hit.
Sometimes the storms are difficult or impossible to avoid. Sometimes the storms are difficult or impossible to explain.
Fear has a way of gripping and bending us in the storms.
Worry can be like the whipping winds surrounding us.

The image of the palm tree under attack in storms and heavy winds reminds me how it feels when we experience the consequences of living in a sinful world, or the enemy attacking us. How comforting it is when we focus on the finished work of Jesus and as believers to be able to apply this knowledge to our lives. No matter what the challenges are, it's nothing in comparison to God's power and blessing in our life. We can be bent and shaken up but God opened up the way for us to live victoriously, not through our own strength but because of His strength and power in us. When the storms are over, we are not only able to recover ... but also to stand upright again, even stronger than before ... all because of our amazing God. I love to be reminded that every weakness in me is an opportunity for God to show His strength through me.

You will have already noticed that God uses trees to speak to me a lot! There are so many analogies, or word pictures, that help me to understand aspects of life, using trees. I have images of trees scattered around the walls of my house, I even have a tree necklace that I wear. Both remind me to remain deeply rooted in Christ and that He is my support network. In Him I am grounded and need to keep 'growing down.' Another saying I like is, *'The deeper the roots, the greater the fruits.'* Being rooted in Christ helps us not be gripped by worry or comparison. If we want to be people deeply planted in faith, women (and men) who can bend and not break when the strong winds of life try to blow us over; I believe that we must get to know Him — to have faith in Him — to spend time in His presence, submit to Him and trust in Him with every part of our lives.

My mum knows I love trees too, which is why she emailed me a devotional that she came across one day. It said, "*A tree that's planted in a rainforest is never forced to extend its roots downward in search of water. As a result, it remains poorly anchored and can be toppled by even a moderate wind. By contrast, the mesquite tree that's planted in a dry desert is threatened by its hostile environment. How does it survive? By driving its roots down thirty feet or more into the earth, seeking water. By adapting and adjusting to harsh conditions, the well-rooted tree becomes strong and steady against all assailants.*" (http://thewordfortoday.co.za/we-are-trained-by-our-troubles)

Sometimes just like we want our own lives to be void of problems or obstacles, so too do we wish this for our children. The old quote that says, 'A mother is only as happy as her unhappiest child' rings so true for me. I find it very difficult to remain joyful when my children are sick, injured or have their feelings hurt in some way. When they are sad, I feel sad too. But like this devotional passage went on to point out, "*Children who have learned to conquer their problems are better anchored and better able than those who have never faced them.*"

Our task, therefore, is to try not to 'helicopter parent' them, hoping that we can control every little thing and avoid any challenges they may face in their lives, but to help them through their struggles. The devotional reading mum sent, said we can do this by *"encouraging them in their distress, intervening when the threat becomes overwhelming, and being available when the crisis comes."* In other words, providing *"them* the tools with which to handle the inevitable problems and pressures of life." Helping to steer them towards God and teaching them to anchor their lives in Him so that when times are tough, they will not topple and fall either.

Leaning on Him

At the beginning of 2019, my daughter experienced a very painful incident when she fell down an uneven curb near our house and badly broke three bones in her leg. She cried. And I cried. But the hardest part was watching her struggle. The pain that she went through was incomprehensible to me. I have never broken any bones, and there was not only the pain of the accident, but also the long-drawn-out pain of more than six months of recovery.

Encouraging her to journal and seek what God was saying to her through this experience, she came up with a few things that had spoken to her throughout her recovery; but what I loved was the image of her learning to lean ... not just physically on her crutches, or even on her friends and family, but watching how she learnt to lean on God. With her permission, I want to include her words as an encouragement in this season, as it reflects much of what autumn is about: strength, resilience, dealing with change, lesson-learning, gaining greater perspective and facing challenges head-on.

~

My name is Eliana and I am currently 12 years old. When I fell and broke 3 bones in my leg, it was very upsetting for me and I had to immediately pull out of many activities that I was involved in like my dance classes, the girls' soccer team and lots of other things that my friends and family were doing.

After two months on crutches, I had a checkup at the hospital to see if I could start walking again, but the x-rays showed that my bones were still broken. My doctor told me that I would most likely not be able to put any weight on my leg for another 3-4 months. I was really upset. My family helped to comfort me. We tried not to become discouraged but instead keep praying and expecting healing in my leg before the next appointment, 6 weeks away. Every day we asked God to miraculously heal my bones.

As the time got closer for my next checkup, I felt both excited and worried. When fear and doubt started to creep in, my parents reminded me that nothing is impossible for God. At my appointment I nervously waited for the x-ray results. My doctor announced that the bones were all healed! Praise God!

The doctor said that I could start putting weight on my leg and begin learning to walk on it. Although I was thankful for the good news, it has taken me much longer to walk 'normally' again than I would like. My heel is sore and my leg muscles feel weak. I get exhausted and frustrated every day.

My favourite verse throughout these past months has been Philippians 4:6, which says, "Don't worry about anything, but in all your prayers, ask God for what you need, always asking with a thankful heart."

I hope that people reading this, who may also be going through a tough time in their life, would also come to know that you can trust God throughout any hard times you go through. Sometimes we look at the problems and things in our life that aren't going how we wanted them to go, when we actually need to be changing our perspective, and handing our burdens to Jesus. And we need to see God's hand in all the details of our lives.

Also, the story in Luke 24:13, when two of the disciples were walking along, talking about the things that were going wrong. Then Jesus appeared to them, but they were so distracted, that they didn't recognise He was walking with them. This showed me that if I get caught up in the setbacks, or problems happening to me, they will keep me from recognising that God is with me, and that He is at work.

I saw this in my life when I broke my leg, because I would feel sad and annoyed about the problems, setbacks, and pain in my leg. Instead of being discouraged, I should have been thankful for the things that I was still able to do, like going to a competition in another country, being able to act in two plays, having the opportunity to help choreograph a dance at my school, and many more blessings from God.

Throughout this season, I have learnt that instead of focusing on the problems that are happening in my life, I need to keep looking at the blessings I have, and I need to keep being positive, so that I can recognise what God is doing around, through and in me.

~

During this autumn season in my daughter's life, my family and I saw her cope with her difficult circumstances, and overwhelming feelings, by leaning on God, asking Him for what she needed, remaining thankful, and not focusing on her problems but on the One who has all the answers.

Facing Challenges

We've all heard the saying, 'Sometimes bad things happen to good people' but in the arena of child trafficking, bad things happen to innocent children, to the vulnerable, the weak, the frail, the defenseless — the ones who needed protecting the most. We are fully aware. It's why we came. As a parent, with three of my own children, I find myself constantly planning and evaluating, limiting risk, protecting, sheltering, watching and doing EVERYTHING in my power to ensure that my children are safe. That nothing 'bad' happens to them. Sometimes though ... no matter how careful we are, how much we do, how much we watch them, how much we eliminate risk — something happens that not even we could predict or foresee. And it knocks us down. Like the force of a strong wind. Suddenly left wondering, how did we end up here? Winded, shocked.

Parents — mother / father — if this is you right now, let me tell you I've been there, too. In that place of questioning ... confusion, anger, shock. I don't have an explanation that will ever make sense of the pain you're in right now. But I will share with you the only thing that got me through and that was focusing on what I *did* know, what I chose to believe and the foundation I stood firmly on. God's word. The truth.

My emotions were all over the place. My mind was telling me all sorts of false things and fear was raging. But my friend, let truth wash over you today and pick you up from the floor. John 10:10 has been one of our family's most recited verses since coming to Thailand. We share it every time we talk about ZOE. I've taught it in the classroom. Our children know it well. And so, I intentionally speak it out. And I believe He is good. And His plan is for life to the fullest. And then I continue to bless the Lord, oh my soul. I worship His holy name. And even when I can barely muster the words and I'm whispering through tears, still ... still my soul will sing His praise unending —10,000 reasons for my heart to sing.

Find those 10,000 reasons each and every day. Maybe it's your small child bashing the rubbish bin lid with a knife shouting, "My God is greater. My God is stronger. God you are higher than any other..." Maybe for you it's cuddling on the couch, an encouraging email, the butterfly that landed on your windowsill, the daisies growing in the yard, the smell of the ocean or getting a letter in the mail ... whatever it is, you can find those 10,000 reasons when you choose to look with a grateful heart and you stand on truth. He never left you. He will carry you through this, and His plan is good.

We don't get much mail here in Thailand, so one day when I saw that there *was* something in our letterbox, I ripped open the envelope immediately and found a card that instantly warmed my heart.

In this day and age of 'instant' EVERYTHING ... I discovered a gem in the way of a delightful message, written in a small farmhouse in an Australian country town named Yackandandah. Sometimes in the seasons of autumn, we find joy and appreciation in the most unlikely places and in some of life's simplest things. Have you ever played in piles of fallen autumn leaves? Ever noticed how the sun casts a golden glow over the changing rust-coloured landscape?

Autumn is a time for gathering and thankful reflection. My husband's nana was a very special lady. She's gone to be with the Lord now, but in March 2018, she celebrated 90 years of life.

As she had done many times before, 'Big Nana', as she was known, sat and scribed words in her beautiful old-style cursive handwriting that had found their way straight into my heart. In a year that I'd found it hard to call, email or even text my friends and family for important occasions, this lovely grandma, on another side of the world, was still thinking and penning out a message to her grandson and his family — despite the fact that they lived all the way over in Southeast Asia. That was just so precious to me.

At that time, as I reflected on the year past, I realised there were many things that *I would actually like to forget.* Things that *hadn't* happened, that *never* succeeded, that *didn't* get finished (or even started) and had *not* turned out as I would've liked. Alternatively, I could choose to acknowledge that although things had not gone to 'my plan', I would finish the year focusing on (and being content with) all that I had in my life and God's love for me. Through the tears, the questions, the frustrations and the anger; there was also so much blessing and laughter. There had been friends who'd encouraged me right when I needed it. There had been answers to prayers, healing and joy. There had been dancing and singing and giggles. There had been birthday celebrations, weddings and baptisms. Not to mention swimming and feasting and snuggling with books on the couch. That year had been enriched with wobbly teeth, growth spurts, timetables learnt, ears pierced and laces tied. When I looked at the year just that bit more closely, I could see what God had done and I was in awe. His faithfulness never ceased. With every sorrow, loss, disappointment and challenge, He had doubled my blessing and mission.

With new seasons ahead, we never know whether they will be 'easy' or 'hard' but we can be thankful for what God is doing in and through us in the unlikely places and find joy in life's simplest things.

When we moved out of the transitional home at the end of 2016, it was one of those times that I look back on now and I'm not really sure how we managed to make it all work. I only *started* packing a few days before we were to move out, I was helping organise a Christmas party for the ZOE missionaries, arranging a Christmas market for my children's school, planning a birthday party for the day after our move and all the while there were several other emotional circumstances that all took place in the same week. During moments of solitude and worship, I tried to meditate on the words of one of my favourite songs at the time. It gave me the perspective that I needed not to be overwhelmed by my circumstances but instead to be overwhelmed by Him — my Creator and my God. It's comforting to me to remember that the pressures, deadlines, meetings, events, appointments and strains in a busy season seem to fade in comparison to how amazing and wonderful He is.

We've moved house a lot so by now, I know very well what is involved. Each time we shift house, I get to sort through tubs, drawers and baskets deciding what we will keep and what we will get rid of. Emotionally speaking, I have boxes of stuff too. These boxes aren't labelled 'laundry,' 'kitchen' or 'bedroom' though. I have one that is marked 'too hard' and another 'goals' ... you get the idea. Sometimes the 'goals' box even gets put inside the 'too hard' one. Maybe you do this too! In the past, I have thrown things like 'learning Thai,' 'speaking in public' and 'getting to bed early' in my too hard box. And mostly, the things I pack in this box stay there for a very long time.

Did you know that studies reveal that as few as 8% percent of people actually keep their New Year's resolutions? Why is it so hard to achieve the goals we set, whether they are big or small? Well, after doing quite a lot of reading on this topic, there were many different theories and suggested solutions attempting to answer this very question. Some say, it's not the goal but the process that's the problem. Others say that you won't create change until you're really ready. Some people say that the goal needs to be specific. So, what is it? Mind over matter? Timing? Preparation? The process? Motivation?

Sorry ... I don't have a definitive answer, but I did hear something interesting recently that made a lot of sense to me. I hear the word 'integrity' talked about a lot. It's one of ZOE's core values and something that all of us are tested on and develop daily. It's doing what you said you were going to do when you said you were going to do it. So, what I heard being shared, was the idea that we often show integrity towards other people, but not ourselves.

Have you ever tried something and failed? Multiple times, right? You've said to yourself, "Starting tomorrow ... I'm going to ... " Why is it that we find it easier to honour promises we make to other people more than to ourselves? The speaker went on to say that our self-integrity and our dignity are closely linked. When we make a commitment to ourselves and fail, our dignity takes a hit. We feel like a failure, like we will never be able to achieve. After committing to things over and over — it's easy to see how our dignity (the way we feel about ourselves, our confidence, self-love etc.) starts plummeting. Our self-esteem suffers, and keeps deteriorating gradually, when we don't practise self-integrity. When we break a commitment to ourselves, or go back on a promise we made, it's not showing self-integrity. Often when we set goals, we start by saying *"I'm going to do this and this ..."* (listing so many things); but to build self-integrity we need to start with one small commitment to ourselves and only when we can keep that, then we can make another one.

To the person who said they were going to lose weight, stop yelling at their kids, quit sugar or start saving money but now feels like they've hit rock bottom with no dignity or self-respect, how do they get back up? One commitment at a time. The way forward is by creating a path of small successes. Commit to making your bed every day, washing the dishes as soon as dinner's done ... whatever it is ... but start to build back trust in yourself. And don't say you'll do something that you're not able to do because the goal is to succeed when you practise self-integrity. After a while when you feel good about the small challenges you've completed, your self-esteem will improve and you will develop the muscle of self-trust instead of self-sabotage.

Over the years, I began to wonder what would happen if I looked in my 'too hard' box and rescued a couple of things out. What if I gave some of these things another chance and tried them one more time? What if ... what if I started Thai lessons again ... what if exercising became a part of my daily routine ... *what if?*

My word for 2017 was 'brave.' It was the year I turned 40 and I am happy to report that *some* of the things that I had previously deemed to be too hard were actually salvaged and re-examined that year. I am pleased to say that I learned the basics of reading and writing in Thai, started exercising more regularly, I spoke in front of many churches in Australia and even I let fish nibble at my ticklish feet (which was something I had said I would never be able to do).

Maybe you don't have a 'too hard' box like me but if you do, I encourage you to grab something out and give it another go. Choose something small to start with. Befriend that neighbour. Make that difficult phone call. Stay calm in the face of a distressing situation. Apologise! I do hope that each week I can keep taking things out of mine bit-by-bit, and not just stuff it full of life's challenges again.

My Personal Trainer

When the first wave of covid hit in February/March 2020, like a lot of people, we found ourselves working from home, overseeing our children's online schooling challenges and we witnessed life completely change from anything we had experienced before. Months of ZOOM calls, lockdown, curfews, and only leaving home for basic necessities all felt so restrictive; but it was also an opportunity to see some of the constraints as advantages in disguise.

For me, I wanted to make sure that I used the time to be productive and to set up some healthier habits that I had been struggling to maintain. There were several factors that helped me establish a new fitness routine during this time that I have continued to protect, even after returning to work in-person and through the ups and downs since. I am hoping that what was established during that time in lockdown will continue to be important to me. After spurts of attempting to achieve fitness goals in the past, I think the difference this time was that I reached a point where it felt less like a 'goal' and more like a 'way of life', which is why I am feeling optimistic about the habits I formed.

During Thailand's third-wave of covid in early 2021, my son was completing a PE assignment and asked me if he could interview me. My kids have been so encouraging to me on my fitness journey and watched me go from walking, to jogging, to running as well as increasing my strength and overall health. It was with great joy that I agreed to answer his questions and as I reflected, I shared with a sense of accomplishment at how far I had come.

He asked me how I stayed motivated to remain fit. I thought back to all the episodes of 'Extreme Weight Loss' I had watched with trainers Chris and Heidi Powell. In the beginning, they became my 'personal trainers' as I fought through the feelings of wanting to give up during a workout, or worse, quitting 'exercise' altogether. As I walked on the treadmill, I watched the contestants on the show struggle to learn to love themselves, set healthy boundaries, face long-term fears as well as confront issues and hurts in their lives that had held them captive, food addictions and other unhealthy choices.

"I think of the promises I have made to myself to be fit and healthy" I answered my son. "I feel better after exercising, so I try to remind myself about that, when I feel less motivated."

Then he asked me what advice I had to maintain an active lifestyle. "My advice would be to start doing something even if it's small." I remembered how in the beginning, I had committed to exercise each day. It was just walking up and down my street, but it was a start. I learnt how to practise self-integrity in those early days, forming habits and doing what I said I was going to do.

"Try to do it every day" I said "but if you miss a day don't let it trip you up or feel guilty about it. Just start up again the next day. If there are days that you are sick or need to rest, do that — but as soon as you feel better get back into it again."

I have seen the transformation in not only my body becoming stronger, more flexible and having more stamina; but also in becoming mentally stronger too. I found that the more I saw physical changes, the easier it became to make healthy choices regarding what I put into my mouth, and in turn my body actually started to crave more nutritious food and not things that weren't good for me. And as I grew in respect for the effort it took to transform and improve my health and fitness, I also grew in self-control. I was able to deliberately choose and consume 'treats' with a much greater consciousness, and as well as better decision-making skills, than in the past.

In summary of the things that really helped me establish these new patterns, I would say that accountability with a couple of trusted friends was really helpful — having someone to exercise with occasionally or regularly, reading about health and wellness and filling my mind with positive things. And having a 'plan' for the days or the moments when I predicted I might struggle to exercise or eat right. Being organised and making a plan of when and how I would fulfill my commitment to exercise. And learning to be patient! For me, I had slowly put on extra weight over the course of more than a decade of living overseas, so I had to firstly acknowledge that I would not be able to lose that weight in one month! Instead of comparing my progress daily, I looked at how far I had come, and celebrated after one month ... six months ... one year! Transformation happened slowly this way, but 'lasting' habits and a 'way of living' is ultimately what I am aiming for. Finally, I would say if no one else notices, if no one compliments you on your changes, it doesn't matter. You will feel better, trust me. It brings me so much joy to be able to run with my children, to swim in the pool without feeling self-conscious, to be a healthy role model and to be active on family holidays. I have way more energy, think through problems differently and set new goals knowing that what I previously thought was impossible, has been achieved and that I can work towards even harder goals.

God wants to be part of every area of our lives, so this path of wellness had to include Him. I looked up devotional plans about everything from food and health, identity, thinking well, running, faith ... knowing there was no better personal trainer (not even Chris Powell) than Him to be my source of encouragement, power and strength.

Lesson Learning

In 2013, when I was teaching some of the recently rescued children at ZOE who couldn't yet attend regular school, a new student started coming to my English class. Hesitant to participate and having never learnt English before, she quickly withdrew and decided that it was just going to be too difficult. Given the circumstances of her past and remembering my own tearful experiences of learning Thai when we first moved here,

I didn't push the issue, instead agreeing just to let her sit in the room and listen. About a month later, without a word, she started bringing her English book to class again and wanted to join in. I could tell that it was so challenging for her. To pronounce each word was extremely difficult and to remember the new vocabulary seemed impossible.

At about the same time, a staff member organised a Thai tutor to come to the children's home and teach Thai to us foreigners at work. It gave all of us non-Thai speakers the opportunity to learn to read and write Thai during work hours for a period of time. Although I had studied some speaking, this was my first attempt at learning reading and writing and the Thai symbols seemed (equally) impossible for me to learn.

And so, I found myself between these two worlds: Teaching English, where the progress was slow and sometimes left me questioning what was actually achieved and being a learner myself and seeing how gradual my own progress was — causing me to wonder whether I was ever going to 'get it.'

Several months later, I went to teach my English class as usual, but something was different — very different. The girl who I referred to earlier was actually smiling as she recited her reading list with the rest of the class. The boys, who just a few months ago were hiding under the desk, were practicing their words too ... and then all of them did some handwriting and ... participated in the game I'd prepared ... and they even came and wrote some answers (in English) on the board. I nearly had to pinch myself and ask, was this the same class?

Just when I had been asking, "Is it all worth it?" I realised that it was. These children are totally worth the wait. It was the breakthrough that I had been praying for. Where trust had begun and determination took off, a new season unfolded right before my eyes. With my Thai study, I can only hope that my Thai teacher will go home one night, with a sigh of relief and quietly exclaim about me, "It *was* all worth it. She finally got it!"

More lessons were learnt in February 2018. My kids had an eventful few days. On top of it being 'Spirit Week' at school and having to dress up each day; the week began with an athletics meet and filled up with music lessons, an unplanned orthodontist appointment, dance class, drama practice and finishing up with two soccer tournaments for the boys in under 14 and under 10 on consecutive days. Plus they had their normal amounts of homework. At the end of it all, I called Dave and I asked if we could take the kids out to dinner to celebrate.

I was excited by his response and pleased that we were 'on the same page' so to speak. You see we both *knew* that the athletics meet had been a huge disappointment. Our highly active and competitive son had not been given the events that he had his heart set on. The day had not gone as expected and to end it all, there had been confusion with medals being distributed incorrectly and not having enough for all the competitors who had won events.

My eldest son's soccer team, who had experienced an average season of games (winning some and losing some) felt hopeful going into their tournament. After losing their first three games though and missing out on the chance to progress through to the next round, we knew the boys felt sad and frustrated to be ending their season at the bottom.

My daughter had wanted to play soccer too but there hadn't been enough girls in her age group to form a team. I had asked the coach of the under 14 girls if she, and a couple of the other girls, could train with his team. He replied that they could train with them but made it clear that they wouldn't get any game time. For weeks, my daughter attended practices feeling like she wasn't really part of the under 14's and that the younger girls were asked to do the same drill each week, over to the side, out of the way. Despite these feelings though, we saw the way she persisted and kept showing up, knowing full well that she wouldn't actually get to play this season but trying to see the experience as preparation for future years.

Maybe right now you're wondering *what* we actually had to celebrate! There were no victories or medals. No 'man of the match', no 'champions.' Looking at the situation purely in terms of how the world measures success, there could be no real reason to go to dinner and applaud our children, right?

This week though, I endeavored to picture my children more as to how I think God sees them, and less through eyes tainted by 'worldly success' or determined by a 'winner's podium.' I got a glimpse of them in a whole new light. As I reflected on the week, my heart started to well up with emotions. These three precious children had achieved so much more than I had realised. They were learning to deal with setbacks. They were developing characteristics so desperately needed in life like coping skills, emotional resilience, creative thinking, and the ability to work in a team. They were learning that whilst it would have felt good to be triumphant in competing, they could lose graciously too. They were experiencing dealing with disappointment and being able to bounce back. They were starting to understand that 'training hard' doesn't always equal a win (or even getting a game). They were practicing not giving up, even when situations don't go as you expect them to.

As a parent, I was learning too. I was recognising that I can't possibly shield or 'save' my children from life's disappointments. I can only help to guide them to be able to overcome these hardships and setbacks. And I can model it by handling my own disappointments in life with grace, choosing to trust God no matter what.

We did take our children out to celebrate at the end of that week. We celebrated and acknowledged 'grace,' 'resilience,' 'persistence' and 'coping skills.' We cheered our kids on for 'bouncing back' and for 'never giving up.' In these seasons of autumn, we learn to face challenges head-on and learn the lessons we need to before the winter comes.

Preparation

Many years ago when my eldest son was small, he sat on the top bunk bed sobbing. "You're so mean Mum. I'm running away." The words stung but I knew his temporary anger at not being allowed to get his own way would soon subside, and after pausing for a second to be sure that the tone of *my* voice was calm, I offered gently to help him pack (offer refused). I left the room remembering other such occasions when similar heated conversations had taken place when I was a child. The backyard at night had seemed so much bigger than it really was and the darkness so much less inviting than the daylight to a small kid with nothing much in her backpack but a few soft toys.

As I walked away to let my son take care of his 'packing,' I reflected on a time many years ago in Australia when we'd had a particularly angry girl staying with us through the foster care program that we were a part of. How she'd thrown everything she could find down the stairs from the upstairs landing. How her mouth had been literally foaming as she spat out words which revealed a heart that had been broken and mistreated too many times. I gathered her younger sisters and my own two children into one room as I silently prayed and quietly made my way to call our agency, whilst keeping one eye on her as she ventured down our street.

So now all these years later and here I was with my own young son, expressing his frustrations and disappointments in a way that made sense to him: Run away. Go. Escape.

As parents, many of us can share funny stories about our children's running away attempts, and the majority of the time, most kids make it all of about ten strides from the safety-net of home before they come running back into their parent's arms. For some children though, the decision to run is one that can be costly, extremely dangerous and frightening. When ZOE first started working with some increasingly more difficult cases, some of the newly rescued children (in particular the teenage boys) found it very difficult to accept love or even understand the importance of them staying at ZOE. We had many people from around the world joining us in faith as we believed for the money needed to start building a custom-designed protection facility. We desperately wanted these precious children cared for without further danger as they adjusted to a life outside of slavery and oppression, but that involved being loved and cared for — which in many ways was often difficult for them to accept.

In February 2018 after many years of planning and preparation, we finally celebrated the Grand Opening of the brand-new Child Rescue Center.

ZOE founder Michael Hart's speech at the opening explained what ZOE's work is all about:

> *"Everyone here has an important role in making this place a refuge for children in Thailand.*
>
> *These beautiful buildings would be only an empty shell, if they did not have the people who are dedicated to rescuing and restoring child victims.*
>
> *All of us here today, can turn these rooms into 'safety,' 'peace' and 'hope' for each child.*
>
> *We are on the same team, playing different positions, but we all fight for victory on behalf of the children we serve."*

After a hard day at school or work, where is the location where you are free to be yourself? To laugh, to cry, to reflect, to process and to acknowledge your emotions and thoughts? It's home, right? Usually we can try to 'hold it together' when people are relying on us, when we need to get our job done, finish a test, complete an assignment or manage our everyday tasks. But for most of us, 'home' is a place of safe refuge, unconditional love and limitless acceptance — well it should be anyway!

I was reminded recently about the children whom ZOE has helped to rescue. When they arrive, they've generally had little to no control over their environment and circumstances so, understandably, they experience varying emotions such as: distrust, fear, shame and grief. They may also have injuries, be unwell or arrive addicted to substances. For them to understand that they have reached a place where they are free to be who they were created to be, where they are loved and accepted for who they are, where wounds can heal and joy be restored. It's an overwhelming experience and one that is often hard to believe.

As I stood in the Child Rescue Center recently, a place where the journey begins, I felt so tremendously grateful — not just for the beautiful buildings, gardens and facilities but for the amazing people who stand ready to embrace these precious children.

In the story of my young son, after waiting for about ten minutes to pass, and feeling sure that his packing must be almost complete, I slipped a tray of food and a drink inside the bedroom door and quietly snuck away. I know his love language is food! And sure enough, a few minutes later, with a sheepish smile and solemn apology, my boy returned to my loving arms.

In seasons of autumn, we need to prepare for the future and for the winter times we know are coming. As parents, we know there are times to correct, boundaries to be set and rules to be taught, but when a child returns back into our arms, there is a beautiful feeling of unconditional love and acceptance that is exchanged and momentarily all else fades to insignificance.

The buildings at ZOE are meant to be white, which is challenging because the soil on the land where ZOE is built is a deep, rich red-orange color. Oftentimes this red-orange dirt gets onto our clothes, cars, and shoes and it is really hard to keep things clean.

As I arrived at work one day, I noticed that there were a couple of guys painting around the front entrance to the building, so I needed to make a detour and go to my office a different way. Some days it was possible to walk around their tools or bamboo scaffolding but mostly, while the work was being done, it all looked like a bit of a mess.

It's not only the buildings at ZOE that need maintenance though; my life, those I work with, the parents, and of course the children themselves — we are all a work-in-progress and sometimes, everywhere I look there is much work to be done. It all just seems like a bit of a mess.

As an Enneagram* Type 7 person I like to experience life to the fullest, but I avoid pain. So, the idea of entering into chaos and mess is often not natural for me. But God is helping me to enter in more fully and "*be*" with others in the same way that He is with me. I am continually amazed at the ZOE staff and parents though, who commit wholeheartedly to seeing lives transformed and throwing themselves in 100% to see the hard work being done.

I'm so thankful that God gives us discernment and sensitivity to the needs around us so that at those times when we just want to walk around, go a different way, or avoid the chaos, He is with us and helps us to enter in and "be" with others in the same way that He is with us.

*https://www.enneagraminstitute.com/type-descriptions/

We are loved and accepted, yes, but loved way too much for Him to just let us remain in our pain, shame, guilt, and in our past. He takes those deep, rich red-orange stains and paints them as white as snow. And then that's how He sees us, clean!

Every time we mess up again and make another stain, He still sees us as righteous! Not because of any good works we can do, but because of Jesus' work on the cross. When we receive Jesus, we receive His righteousness. And it's not a process like painting a building, it doesn't fade over time or wear out based on our performance. It's a beautiful reminder of our God who forgives us and gives us a new life and a pure heart. What a wonderful gift!

Perspective

Growing up, it was normal for my family to eat dinner together every night. My parents set aside the time and place to sit around the table with my siblings and me, sharing in both the meal and our lives. I think these dinner experiences, throughout my childhood, teenage and young adult years, definitely influenced the importance that as a parent, I now place on our family's nightly mealtimes and the choice to not 'just' see them as times of eating food.

If you've ever read through the pages of the Bible, you'll have noticed that there are so many references to food. Between the first book Genesis through to the last pages, food is mentioned over 1,000 times. Jesus spoke many times about being hungry and thirsty and is Himself called the Bread of Life.

Food is an equalizer. At a very basic level, we all need to be fed. But just like food, I believe all of us need God's grace and forgiveness, too. Every bite of food can remind us that we are dependent on Him. In fact, food is even the symbol used to represent and remember Jesus' sacrifice on the cross. As a believer, when taking communion, it's a reminder of how much God loves me and the sacrifice He made so that I can spend eternity with Him.

When I was a young adult, I used to cringe if people asked me to share my testimony. It started a little something like this, "Well I grew up in a Christian home ... " which, to be honest, at the time, I thought sounded quite boring. It was not like the other testimonies that I would hear shared at church from a transformed drug addict or someone who'd been in a gang until they met God and He totally changed their life. Naively, at one stage, I even started wishing I had a testimony like that. I wondered how the story of a young girl who accepted Jesus with a child-like faith on the back steps at her house, could ever really impact anyone compared to the wild testimonies from those who had been saved from really 'bad' past experiences.

What I had failed to understand back then was that 'sin is sin.' My sin may not have made its way to a juvenile courtroom, but it was no better or worse than anyone else's. It says in Romans 3:23 that, 'all have sinned and fall short of the glory of God.' Which means that my testimony is not even about me ... it is about what God did when He sent His son Jesus 'for me.'

After gaining this new perspective and being a parent myself, I have changed my thinking and, if I hear about someone who grew up in a Christian home like mine, who knew Jesus at an early age and who never 'fell away' or backslid, then I praise God just as much as when I hear the dramatic rescue stories. Either way we all need Him. He doesn't love me because I'm good, He loves me because ... *He is good!*

If ever I am tempted to feel like my testimony is 'boring' because I never found myself homeless, addicted to drugs, or in jail, I remember that my testimony is about what He has done for me, not about anything I have done. Now after all these years, I give glory and thanks to God for the life I have. I am learning to never let anyone, including the enemy, allow me to think that my testimony is less than amazing, lame, or not worth sharing. My testimony reflects a love story of someone sacrificially giving His life for mine. And of the only One who can truly nourish and deeply satisfy the desires of my heart to be loved and accepted.

If this rings true for you too, then know this — your testimony counts! Your testimony is awesome and it's powerful ... because of what *He* did!

Even in the worst possible scenarios that ZOE has been involved in, we have seen how God can tenderly take which was stolen, broken, or rejected and radically change, restore and reclaim it. He did not cause the pain of the children rescued, but He will not waste it. He makes all things new and beautiful ... in His time. (Ecclesiastes 3:11)

Whatever our backgrounds are, may God always receive the glory from our testimonies of redemption, provision, and protection. I thank God so much that I had parents who knew the power of prayer. Who got down on *their* knees and committed *my* life to His care. I believe that we serve an amazing God with unlimited power to heal and save, just as He did in Bible times.

Changing Course

For anyone who has used a GPS (predating Google Maps), you will be familiar with that voice that announces, *"RECALCULATING"* when you go off route and start heading in a new direction for a while. The GPS is such a wonderful device though, isn't it? Like how it knows where you're headed and sets a new way of getting there.

At the end of the school year in June 2013, there was a teaching position available at the small school where our three children attended. Although I knew how great the need was, I did not apply for it or feel at peace about it at the time, because I felt that full-time work would probably not be a wise choice for our family at that stage. In our final week of visiting

Australia though, I received a couple more emails from the staff explaining that they had still not found a teacher for the Grade 2-3 class and that school was soon to start back. This was the class that two of my children were going to be in.

One day, I had just been a regular mum dropping off her three children at school, helping out once a week with Literacy rotations and doing other small jobs and then, before I knew it, the Grade 2-3 vacancy was filled by the only parent left standing on the sidelines holding a teaching degree ... you guessed it! Me! I said I never wanted to homeschool and I guess this technically wasn't homeschooling since I went *to* the school and I taught my children there, but it definitely was not what I had planned!

What had started out as a one-year obligation though, soon turned into a one-year blessing. What an amazing opportunity it was to teach not only two of my own children, but all their friends too. When I first started helping out at the school once a week, I worked with a boy who was in Grade 1 at the time, who had reading and spelling difficulties. He tried so hard but the progress was slow. Now in Grade 2, he was still a very weak reader and although he had good ideas for story writing, he was unable to reread his own writing or even tell me what he'd written. After mentioning to his parents that I thought he needed to be assessed for dyslexia, an online test was all that they could afford. The test indicated that dyslexia was an issue, but I realised with limited resources that all I could do was believe in this boy, try my best to support him and keep encouraging him to 'never give up.'

Together with some of the other teachers, we began to find ways that we could help this boy (as well as other students) who struggled with sensory processing, autism, English as a second language amongst the other challenges of living in a transient community — many of them being third culture kids and being far away from their country of birth.

What took place in the space of just one year amazed me. From the brain gym exercises every morning, the use of fuzzy boards and other spelling activities that involved multisensory learning ... to making up songs, which helped students remember grammar, Bible verses and timetables ... it was only as I began to assess and write reports in the final term that I truly understood the progress that had been made. The boy with dyslexia, who had been below Grade 1 level at the beginning of Grade 2 in reading, was now at the high end of Grade 2. He had joined the other children in the class with their spelling lists and in fact felt confident to answer *their* questions on how to spell words correctly. I could not stop thanking God for this amazing opportunity to see this boy's transformation.

The other amazing things in that year included seeing the class's strong desire to share their work in front of the other classes each Friday at Chapel. They were so enthusiastic and proud to showcase what they'd written each week. Sometimes I would overhear their conversations as they sat quietly whispering about in which country they were going to be a missionary when they grew up ... "I'm going to Africa," "I'm going to be taking Bibles into China," another would reply. This class loved life. They loved to sing, worship God and pray. Their faith inspired me. They prayed for each other's needs daily and they saw answers to their prayers. This class with its mix of cultures and languages loved opportunities to learn and question and respond. They loved learning about people who have made a difference in the world and who never gave up. Their verbal and written responses to people like Nick Vujicic, Mother Teresa, Corrie Ten Boom, Bethany Hamilton, George Mueller and many others, were beyond their years.

Sometimes 'autumn' throws us changes in plans that we have to deal with. Sometimes the route we thought we were taking turns out to lead us to somewhere else; but through complete trust in God, I have seen time and time again how He takes all sorts of *'recalculating'* situations and uses them to bless us, not ever wasting a single experience.

For example, one day, after I had been telling my sister on the phone how excited I was with my new 'magic mop' — I know — probably not many other people get excited about their mops, but I do! I mentioned that I would try to make her a video showing how it worked. So, after I had swept through the house, I got my mop and bucket and set to work making her the video showing how the magic mop spins and fits under things, etc. I was actually feeling quite proud of my video efforts until I discovered later that a simple 'Google' search brought up numerous more-professional videos than the one I made ... of course it does!! Oh well.

What was strange though was that a couple of months after making the video, I had been commenting to Dave about how I thought our kitchen floor had lost its shine. It was so weird, but even after mopping and mopping, once it had dried, it was 'cloudy' looking again. Clean, but not shiny ... so sad. With all that in mind, one day I decided that my mission was to get that kitchen floor back to a dazzling shine. After mopping it a few times using the normal floor wash (maybe I needed reminding about the definition of insanity — doing the same thing and expecting different results) it still looked dull. So, I knew it was time to try some other remedies. I tried a liquid soap-vinegar-baking soda mixture first, and when that didn't work, I used dish soap and vinegar ... and then I went to just vinegar and warm water. It was clean and slightly less cloudy after all my mopping experimentation, but still nowhere near what it should've looked like. I was baffled. Then, all of a sudden, I remembered *the end* of the conversation Dave and I had, where he had said ... "maybe your mop needs a new mop head." Surely not?! I mean I knew the house had been filthy when we moved in but we hadn't had the mop *that* long. So, off I went to search through my cleaning supplies and sure enough, there was a spare mop head. I figured out how to take the old one off and that's when I noticed the difference in the colour between the two mop heads ... what? Crazy!! Eww!

With the head replaced, I set to work with renewed enthusiasm and optimism and, sure enough, the floors began to shine again. Just like that! Amazing. As I was gladly mopping away, music playing and happy thoughts now running through my mind, I had one of those 'aha' moments about my mop and how our family's life had kind of been a bit like the mop, too.

Have you ever had those times in your life when everything seems to be going okay? The kids seem settled, your marriage is strong, work is enjoyable, everything is sort of 'going to plan' so to speak, when suddenly or even not so suddenly ... maybe subtly, you stop and wonder, what happened? Why aren't my kids thriving? Why are we arguing about these issues? Am I really where I am meant to be? Sometimes we can get so used to doing things 'the good old way,' 'the safe way' or just the 'same way' we always have.

Like me with the mop head, there can come times in life when it suddenly dawns on you that 'umm ... actually that's just not working anymore.' And you ask yourself, "Why doesn't it look nice and shiny anymore?" You know you're still cleaning the same way you've always done. You're using the same cleaning products that have never let you down before ... but now suddenly the shine is gone and you just don't know why.

Oftentimes we can go round and round questioning, what's wrong with the floor, why isn't it shiny? Why? Why? Why? All the while mopping it again and again in the same way hoping that things will improve until you suddenly look at the situation in a new way, seeing that what is required to fix the problem is actually something totally different than what you had thought.

During the seasons of autumn, I find myself replacing metaphorical mop heads in 'life.' There needs to be adjustments made and then finally things start to look shinier again. When situations get a little bit too 'cloudy,' autumn is a great time to modify, correct, face challenges head-on and fine-tune things until the problems are fixed. Maybe it's just me and my 'magical mop' analogy, but I am so glad that there is always God's truth — the Word — in my life to guide me and whisper softly to me when my mop gets dirty, "It's time to change what you're doing!"

Just remember though (and I'm preaching to myself now) that when the shine seems to have disappeared, and nothing seems to be working; we must not fall into the trap of trying to make everything appear shiny again in our own strength. To be honest, there have been times when David and I have doubted our effectiveness here and we've wondered if we can really do enough to impact and help all these children. But what we're realising is that, if we rely on our own strength, it will never be enough. So instead of feeling discouraged by the size of the task, we are learning that it is these times that we can be encouraged by the limitless power of our God. Thankfully, God, who is all-powerful, cares about the individual and He most definitely cares about children. It is only through His almighty power that we can do anything. And sometimes all we *can* do is to fall down on our knees with an overwhelming conviction that we must continue to pray for and uplift those who are suffering.

Complacency

Growing up we had many Bibles in our home. My parent's faith was real and unswerving. I saw their prayers answered all throughout my childhood. And I never had a doubt as to whether God was real or not because I felt His presence and I saw evidence of His work in the lives around me and in my own life. I felt God respond to my prayers, closing doors at times, telling me to 'wait' or saying 'yes' and providing for me. I always felt that God was near and even when I didn't, I knew that it was me who had moved — not Him.

I was in church from the time I was born and enjoyed years as part of a vibrant children's church ministry. I went to Bible camps, youth groups and overall, I was a fairly 'good' girl. I had an adventurous spirit. I liked to push the boundaries and question my parents' seemingly strict rules or decisions but at the end of the day, I wanted to please them and not purposely make wrong choices or go against their instructions.

As a young married woman at 21 years old, this solid faith base that I had been given through my childhood years was a strong foundation. I recognised early on Dave and I were two imperfect people coming together, but that God was my strength. Even though our marriage was really good, I had somewhat of an understanding even back, then that my identity, worth and approval could only be found in God — not my family, husband or friends.

Reflecting back, I am trying to remember what the health of my spiritual life was really like back then, but it's hard to recall. David and I were definitely going to church, serving, attending small groups, doing courses, praying, etc. But at the end of 2003, when we were preparing for a big trip that we'd been saving up for ... to the U.K., Europe and U.S.A; I remember being faced with an interesting choice. We were going to be going away for five-and-a-half weeks. We had one large backpack and a small carry-on each. We were heading into the northern hemisphere's winter, so we had to be selective about what to take with limited space. Our bags were packed tight and I remember having this inner dilemma about whether to take my Bible or not. Now, for the younger generation here, this was the early 2000's before smartphones and YouVersion! Anyway, looking back, I must not have been in the habit of reading my Bible daily because I ended up deciding to leave it behind in the end.

Off we set on December 13, 2003, for the trip of a lifetime. With high expectations, we were ready to embrace adventure, and new experiences, every step of the way. After a few days exploring London, we made our way to the Royal National Hotel to begin a ten-day Contiki tour around Europe. At 7:30 am we left with our group and headed to the White Cliffs of Dover where we caught a small cruise ship across the English channel to France. Once we arrived there, we headed for Belgium, Brussels, the Netherlands and at 5:30 pm, after a lot of travelling, we arrived in Amsterdam.

Over the next ten days, we saw some of the most incredible places in the world. Our experiences were so over-the-top-crazy-good and really, we were bombarded with sensory overload every single day. From the sights, smells, sounds, tastes, the cultures, the languages ... everything was new, different and amazing. And the people we met along the way were absolutely lovely.

There were some downsides to our tour though, which we tried hard not to let discourage us; but by the end of the trip, these incidents did amount to some frustration. It started with small things like running late and arriving in countries after dark, followed by having to leave really early the next morning without having the chance to explore. Then in Switzerland we got stuck at the top of Mount Pilatus in 100km winds meaning they couldn't run the cable car and take us back down. In the scheme of life, it is not too bad being stuck on the top of a stunningly beautiful mountain in the Swiss Alps, but the problem for this huge Sound-of-Music-fan was that it meant we missed going to Austria, which had been one of the places I had most wanted to see. After that, we had to play catch-up with our trip so we felt even more rushed as the Switzerland delay had put us somewhat behind the already tight schedule. We travelled through Venice, Florence and Rome spending a wonderful (cold) Christmas Eve at St. Peter's Square in Vatican City. We headed back to Florence on Christmas Day and then from being in Italy one day, we went on to Nice in France after that. After only rinsing select clothes items, we were finally able to put some dirty washing out to be cleaned at our hotel, but unfortunately things came back stained ... or ... not at all! After Nice we set off for Lyon but there was something wrong with our bus to the point where it was unable to be driven. After waiting most of the day for a replacement bus, we arrived in Lyon late and again, had only a few hours at night to see anything. Next, we headed to Paris but we were still behind schedule so, after a quick night tour of the city, we arrived at the Eiffel Tower at 10:55 pm, only to find out that it was shut! The next day we were evacuated off a train due to a bomb scare and then our bus was broken into ... and the rest of the other frustrations and setbacks are all a bit blurry now!

After the 10-day tour and a few extra days in London, we set the alarm for 4.00 am to catch a flight to New York. As we sat in the taxi on the way to the airport, my thoughts started to reflect back to the tour of Europe and I felt my annoyance and disappointments starting to resurface. And it all boiled down to this one thing: I understood that most of the let-downs were unavoidable; they weren't all the tour company's fault. But the thing that I felt mad about most was our tour manager's attitude. Although he was generally a nice guy, his outlook every time we would miss something or be late to places was one of being unconcerned and complacent. He had done the tour so many times over years and years, to the point where I felt like he didn't realise that for most of us, if we missed seeing the Eiffel Tower or Austria; we weren't coming back in two weeks' time! This was our once-in-a-life time opportunity!

Now, I've heard God speak to me in different ways before but I have never heard the audible voice of God. As I sat in that London black cab, buried in my thoughts about the missed opportunities, I felt God speak so deeply and directly into my heart, it was like it reached my very core. With words that cut through my own thoughts, I felt Him say, "*That's what you're like.*" Wait! What? God thinks I'm like the tour manager?! And then I felt Him say, "*You're complacent just like him. You've known me your whole life. There are people who have only known me a short amount of time who are more excited about their relationship with me than you are. But you treat me with such indifference —like 'meh!' — thinking, 'God will always be there ... it'll be ok.'*" Wow! That cut me deep! Because it was true.

No one likes times of correction. I believe God does not want us to be sin-conscious and hide from Him like Adam did. He wants us to be righteous-conscious and crawl up close and walk with Him because God fully reconciled us to Himself through the death of His Son (Romans 5:10). So, I knew I didn't need to feel unworthy or that what I'd done was unforgivable. I could really sense that God (who is a good, good Father) was showing me this area of my life from a place of love and for *my* benefit. I tell you though, I have never forgotten that moment! It was so transformative and life-changing for me. Rooting out complacency for me as well as finding and addressing all sorts of other issues along the way, has made my life so much better. When something is brought to the light and exposed, change can occur. He gives us the power, victory and strength to grow in both truth and the understanding of our new nature. His righteousness is at work in us.

Contentment

Dave and I sometimes visit a local restaurant that serves an especially delicious northern Thai curry called *gaaeng hang laeh rnuu* (pork leg stew). It's the sort of dish that we never need a big portion of because the flavours are so intensely deep and rich, that one small serving shared between two people provides enough taste to linger in your mouth and remind you of how satisfying it was for the next few hours. We never leave feeling bloated or too full but (I'm not exaggerating) hours later we can still be heard uttering, "That curry was so delicious!" I appreciate this dish all the more since trying to make it myself a few times. It's quite an effort with a long list of ingredients combining spices and being slow-cooked for a substantial amount of time, to release a wonderfully subtle combination of all the flavours. When made correctly ... seriously! There are no words!

One December, I looked at our calendar with all the upcoming events that our family had either been invited to or were asked to be a part of through work, school, friendships, church and extracurricular activities. It was a lot. Granted, I am more of an introvert nowadays but I really started to feel overwhelmed by it all. The most difficult part was that when I sat down to look at what each thing was (so I could cut a few things out) I was surprised to notice that they were all really 'good' things. Not one of the things, in isolation, was a waste of time, unnecessary or seemed unenjoyable, but all of them together was simply too much.

I was explaining to a friend how I don't like to get to the end of a busy week packed with 'good' things and not even be able to remember what I did a few days earlier. After an event I want to 'savour' it and make space to 'digest' it within our family. I want to give my heart time to respond and to block out the noises that so often deafen me from hearing what it was I needed to learn through each experience.

I have come to appreciate the beauty of the Thai culture in the way they prioritise — stopping and sitting to eat together, in contrast to the deteriorating western 'drive-through' influence — where food is consumed on-the-way-to wherever ... while rushing to the next 'thing.'

Having time to 'chew on,' 'mull over' and reflectively appreciate the moments in life — just like that curry — has become so much more appealing to me than the all-you-can-eat buffet of an overcrowded life. The buffet, from a distance, may aesthetically seem more appealing, but soon enough you're left feeling so full, you can't even remember the first thing you ate. There is nothing wrong with the individual dishes, they're all delicious, but later the flavours have all mixed into one; and the satisfaction that you thought you might have by the end, is tainted by the bloated feelings that leave you feeling like you never want to eat again!

As a parent I often think about this challenge of how I help to navigate my children through this 'buffet-style' of life, guiding them as they grow up with so many all-you-can-eat opportunities. I question how will I effectively and deliberately model a reflective and sensitive approach in my own life? I believe that it is something that we must fight to do ourselves first in order to model it to our children. If I can't insert 'pauses' into my own life that allow me to joyfully experience and reflectively savour the tastes of my day and week, then how can I direct my children, faced with every distraction and opportunity laid before them, to be able to do the same? How can I teach my kids that yes, it may all be good, but that does not mean it must all be consumed? I can't do everything. My children can't experience everything either. Even if every opportunity looks good, our job must be to prevent them, and us, from drowning in activities.

Overcommitment is not what we were made for and it can subtly become an idol or a destructive habit. It's easy to think our identity and worth is in what we 'do' (or what our kids can do) instead of in Christ and being a child of God. In an environment where smorgasbords abound and it all looks so appealing, it can be hard to say no to opportunities, invitations and new ideas. But when we become too busy (even doing good things) we crowd out our ability to 'pause' and hear God's voice and we miss out on the intensely deep and rich moments in life. I guess, as the saying goes, sometimes less is more.

When we sense that autumn is coming to an end and winter is on its way, we must start to prepare ourselves for what's next. You know the beautiful, strong palm tree that I wrote about earlier, that so magnificently portrays strength, resilience and coping with changes? It does have one weakness.

Palm trees are vulnerable to damage from freezing. "Palm trees generally become dormant in cool weather, such as from late fall through winter. This means that their growth slows down or stops until warm weather returns. It's a survival technique they use to get through the inhospitable cold season." (homeguides.sfgate.com) What's more is that cold snaps (weather below the normal range of temperature) can in fact kill palm trees. So just like we need to understand how particular trees and plants grow, what their needs are, and how to protect *them* in really severe weather; more importantly we need to understand how to prepare and protect ourselves.

Let's start by asking a few questions. Where is my warmth, energy and power going to come from? If I am only relying on my own strength, what happens when it depletes? What do I need to clear out or get rid of before winter hits? Is there forgiveness, repentance or new boundaries that need to be put in place? What do I need to put on and what do I need to get rid of?

Autumn can be an amazing season of change and readiness. We can be strengthened in the 'autumns,' equipped and well-prepared for challenges that may be ahead. Remember the virtuous, honorable woman spoken about in Proverbs 31? When I wrote that she had no fear of winter, I do think it's because she knew God had her family 'covered' in their time of need. But I do also think that the 'Proverbs 31 woman' was productive and anticipated what her family would need and set to work doing what she could do to face the winter as well-prepared as possible, but simultaneously *knowing* that her trust and her strength was completely in Him. It is in light of all this that I started to understand that not one single day of the autumn seasons in my life: the planning, the preparation, the lesson learning, the clearing out, and all the other experiences I had, were ever a waste. When it seems as though life is overwhelming, 'recalculating' or our prayers seem to be going unheard, we must not feel discouraged. God uses this season to remind us that He is our source of power and strength.

Discussion Questions

Comparing the palm tree and your struggles, can you think of a time when you felt like you were being 'bent' through an experience? Would you say that you actually became stronger than what you were before going through this time?

Think about a situation when you needed to be both productive (anticipating what you or your family would need for the future to face a winter season ahead), but that you also knew that your trust and your strength needed to be found completely in God. What's the key to balancing both these things at once?

Think of the analogy of the mop head needing to be changed. In addition to the Word of God, can you identify a trustworthy person in your support network that would help you to recognise when you might need to replace a metaphorical mop head in your life?

Is it easy for you to bounce back from life's disappointments with grace, choosing to trust God no matter what? Is it more natural to celebrate the 'achievements' of yourself and others, or can you see that 'grace,' 'resilience,' 'persistence' and 'coping skills' are also great accomplishments to celebrate? How can you learn to face challenges head-on and learn the lessons you need in this season — before the winter comes?

Do you need to alter the way you view how life is 'meant to be?' Through your seasons of transition, have you ever had the temptation to stop engaging new people/relationships because of the pain of saying goodbye or losing them? Or have you been on the receiving end of people not embracing you?

God uses this season to remind us that He is our source of power and strength. Use the space to write any additional thoughts, verses, encouragements or reflections about autumn here:

Yes! There is such a thing.

-HEALTHY GINGERBREAD-

Guilt free biscuits... yes please!

Ingredients

- 2 tbsp of date paste
- 1/3 cup honey
- 1 tbsp ginger (or more if you want a stronger flavour)
- 1 heaped tsp of pumpkin pie spice*
- 3 tbsp coconut oil
- 1/2 tsp baking soda
- 1/4 tsp salt
- 1 3/4 cups almond flour
- 1/4 cup of tapioca flour (and a bit more for sprinkling on the bench)

*Pumpkin Pie Spice
3 tbsp ground cinnamon
2 tsp ground ginger
2 tsp nutmeg
1 ½ tsp ground allspice
1 ½ tsp ground cloves

Instructions

1. Preheat oven to 170-180 °C.
2. In a saucepan pour honey, spices and 2 tbsp of date paste. Stir together and heat until the edges start to bubble and then remove it from the stove.
3. Stir in the oil. Add the baking soda.
4. In a bowl mix the almond flour, tapioca flour and salt.
5. Add the date and spice mixture to the bowl of flour and combine until you have a smooth dough. You can place the mixture in the refrigerator to cool or roll it straight out.
6. Sprinkle tapioca flour on a clean surface and roll out the dough. Use a cookie cutter to make shapes.
7. Bake on a lined baking tray for about 8-9 minutes.
8. Allow them to cool slightly on the tray before transferring to a cooling rack.

Makes 21 small people.

DATE PASTE
Soak pitted dates in hot water until they are soft.
Food process or blend until smooth, adding a few teaspoons of water as necessary until a smooth paste forms.

This cake is one of my family's favourites.

-PUMPKIN CAKE-

It's perfect for Thanksgiving, Christmas time or any occasion throughout the year.

Ingredients

- 1/4 cup melted coconut oil
- 1/4 cup honey (or maple syrup)
- 1/4 cup coconut sugar
- 1 cup cooked pumpkin
- 4 eggs
- 1 cup almond flour
- 1/4 cup coconut flour
- 1/2 tsp baking soda
- 1 1/2 tsp pumpkin pie spice*
- 1/2 tsp cinnamon
- 1/2 tsp salt

CRUMB TOPPING

- 1/4 cup coconut flour
- 1/2 cup almond flour
- 2 tbsp coconut sugar
- 1/2 teaspoon cinnamon
- 2 tablespoons honey (or maple syrup)
- 2 tablespoons coconut oil

Instructions

1. Preheat oven to 165 °C and line a pan with baking paper.
2. Make the topping first. In the food processor, combine coconut flour, almond flour, coconut sugar, cinnamon, honey (maple syrup), and coconut oil. Pulse so that it's crumby. Put in a bowl and set it aside.
3. In the food processor combine coconut oil, honey (maple syrup), coconut sugar, and pumpkin. Mix well.
4. Add in the eggs and mix until incorporated.
5. Add in the almond flour, coconut flour, baking soda, pumpkin spice, cinnamon, and salt. Mix until no dry pockets remain. Pour into prepared pan and top with crumb topping.
6. Bake for 45-50 minutes. Serve cooled or cold.
7. Store in fridge after the first day (if there's any left).

Oh, and the aroma while it's cooking is delightful! Enjoy.

*Pumpkin Pie Spice
3 tablespoons ground cinnamon
2 teaspoons ground ginger
2 teaspoons nutmeg
1 ½ teaspoons ground allspice
1 ½ teaspoons ground cloves

Hello Winter

'God uses this season to show that He is the One who gives air in our lungs, strength in our legs and a promise of never leaving us.'

One of the first things that I found fascinating upon moving to Thailand was just how different winter was. We left Melbourne's summer in January 2010 and arrived in Chiang Mai's winter. This surprisingly meant lovely mild mornings, blue skies and sunny tops of 30-degrees Celsius. I simply couldn't believe how I would actually love 'winter' weather for the first time in my life.

I can't say that I have enjoyed the metaphorical winters quite as much as actual Thailand ones, but I have been learning that God is good, faithful and unchanging through them all. Though there are times when things in our lives are uprooted, torn down, die or need to be thrown away, on the flipside ... we experience new life, healing, planting, rebirthing and joy.

I think that during the winter seasons it is helpful to remind ourselves to look ahead with expectation knowing that spring will come. It's easy to feel tired in the winter, but while we wait out the cold, it is important to remain alert and learn the lessons that we need to at this time. Only as we begin to grasp what this season is teaching us can we shake off the unnecessary layers that were weighing us down, lay aside *'our'* ways of doing things and step into the newness of what God wants to do in, and through us as we move into the spring.

The Greek philosopher Aristotle said, "To appreciate the beauty of a snowflake it is necessary to stand in the cold." I can't actually imagine holding a snowflake right now or standing in the cold; it seems strange to even be writing about winter on a 40-degree day in Thailand. Of course though, it is winter in the symbolic sense that I refer to in this chapter. And yes, even in the longest, darkest of winters I believe that beauty can be found.

This is the time to grab your scarf and gloves, pull on your thick warm coat and rug-up for a journey through winter. During the storms, when I have tried to appreciate the wonders of winter, I have discovered sweet periods of rest, contemplation, planning, finding God, solitude, being still, renewed hope and increased trust. I have had times where I have felt His strong arms holding me but I have also had to embrace moments of letting go, tearing down, grief, loss and uncertainty.

Some people say that you never appreciate the spring until you've been through a tough winter. But there are also beautiful lessons of faith to be learnt in the coldest, darkest moments of life too. Just because something is hard does not mean it is not good. There will be challenges and loss in the winters of life, but we can choose to find joy in the hardships and learn to trust God's goodness through even the coldest, darkest season.

A Time to Die

On October 13, 2016, an immeasurable depth of grief broke out in Thailand with the announcement that the beloved King Bhumibol Adulyadej had died at the age of 88. As a foreigner living in Thailand, it was a time to show respect, sensitivity and to stand alongside our Thai friends, neighbours and colleagues with compassion and thoughtfulness. Their king, who was the world's longest-reigning monarch at that time, was a source of stability for the people of Thailand, and each one of them felt the loss greatly. The vast majority had no memory of any other king.

As a year-long period of mourning was declared, everyone in Thailand began wearing dark colours, websites changed their tones to black and white, and television channels were switched to royal documentaries. 'Festivities' were avoided for at least the first 30 days and even after that they were much more subdued than normal. The government sector observed a year of mourning, under which civil servants wore black for the entire time. In a land where colours have such a profound meaning, people only resumed wearing their regular clothes when the mourning period officially ended on midnight of October 30, 2017.

Parts of our journey through life will include times of sadness, inner turmoil, questioning and grief. What we can learn in these times is how to respond in the right way. As challenges are thrown at us, we can learn to set our minds on things above, guard our thoughts, embrace the promises of God, walk out our faith. It's easy to accept life when we actually *like* the plan, right? But what happens when we can't understand what's happening? Will we still trust Him in the dark when we cannot see the way out? I was challenged by these thoughts many years ago when I read the book, *Raising a Soul Surfer* written by Cheri Hamilton whose daughter, surfer Bethany Hamilton, lost her arm in a shark attack.

I was equally challenged when a young man (Mimi) from ZOE suddenly became ill. He was a ZOE leadership student and had been a previous employee at ZOE. Mimi and his young wife, they had their whole lives ahead of them, but sadly he passed away unexpectedly right before our eyes. Or when a former work colleague P'Am (PeeAm) who, while heading off on holidays with her husband, was involved in a terrible car crash and died. Going back even more years prior, two separate friends in their twenties passed away too soon: one from cancer and the other in a work-related accident.

Your winters will look different than mine.

Maybe *your* plan involved having children and it never came to be. Maybe a certain job just never quite worked out. Or a friendship, a family relationship *or* marriage ended up in tatters, broken and seemingly irreparable.

We are led to face a difficult but undeniable reality. Sometimes life seems different from what we expected. So, what happens then? What if all we own is suddenly snatched away, if everything that's familiar to us is removed, if our friends abandon us; if our job is gone, if we no longer have our health or if death takes away those whom we love the most. And these things *do* happen ... to people ... *every day.* It's usually in these winters where I wrestle with these tough questions the most.

As a Christian, one thing that I know about God is that His purposes span the centuries. Psalm 90:1 says, "Lord You have been our dwelling place throughout all generations..." It goes on to say, "from everlasting to everlasting, You are God." I often need to remind myself that God is sovereign and *not* someone *I* control. He knows what He is doing and I must quit looking at the world or myself and instead keep my eyes on Him.

Throughout my life, I am grateful to have witnessed many examples of people, who during their bleakest times, have continued to choose to believe God's promises instead of their own personal thoughts or feelings. People who have honoured God despite their disappointment or pain and yet, through their tears and heartbreak, have chosen to trust. No matter how things looked and no matter how they felt, they had supernatural peace and joy, knowing that God was still in control. When we can submit and trust in His plan, we can be assured that He knows what He is doing and His ways are always best.

A Time to Trust

Corrie Ten Boom's tapestry poem 'Life is But a Weaving' can speak to us in the winter trials as a reminder that no matter what our situation, we have Jesus — Immanuel — God with us. We may not be able to understand what is going on but we can trust that He does.

How did Corrie remain focused on God during the atrocities she experienced during the war — and afterwards, knowing she had lost her family? She trusted that even though all she could see was a jumbled mess of thread, God already knew what the finished artwork would look like. And not one string of experience, good or bad, in her life was wasted. We can also trust that the One, who is weaving it all together, knows precisely what He is doing in our lives.

Listening to a sermon once by Robert Ferguson, I was challenged by his message which was entitled 'Not My Will.' He was talking about the phrase that Christians use a lot which is 'God is good.' He went on to explain that whilst God *is* good, we often elevate 'goodness' above God and, instead of putting Him first in our lives, we make 'good' into a false god. Remember earlier when we defined idols as being any other 'thing' besides God that we set our heart on, which rule us or that we trust.

Which leads us back to the question: do we *really* trust God? Do we trust God when things aren't good? Do we believe that God is good even when things don't end up the way we thought they would? In the winter, I am challenged to choose to believe that God is sovereign *and good* and can be trusted, no matter what happens — good or bad. I once heard it said that "It is not enough to just trust God that what we fear most will not happen." Trust, and faith, in God's promises produce a certain attitude and mindset that is different to the world's, even when faced with challenges. When our Plan A is to trust in God, we don't need a Plan B or C. His faithfulness, goodness and resources never run out. It's having confidence in His character and His Word.

I mentioned Cheri Hamilton earlier, Bethany Hamilton's mother. In her book she writes: *"Before the attack, I had so many plans for my future and dreams of how my daughter's amazing talents could affect the surfing community. But my hopes and dreams were too small for God. He always had much grander plans. Now I am sitting in a movie theatre knowing that our story would go out and reach people who maybe have never even seen an ocean. My plans were way too small. It took a tragedy to shatter them and recast them into God's plans. Bethany's story of faith will be seen in faraway places where she may never get to visit herself... it will go to people and places that would never have heard of Bethany if she had merely become the world champion of women's surfing. When our plans unravel, when the fear and the tears of tragedy collapse our safe and petty world, we can only turn to God who works all things for good to those who love Him. The frayed fabric of our pain becomes a work of beauty in His hands."*

I also love the reflections of singer/songwriter, Natalie Grant who said that she is, "Learning to seek His face, before she seeks His hand. Learning to declare His goodness regardless of the outcome. Recognising once again that it is not what He does, but WHO HE IS." To trust Him, I choose to see life as the tapestry ... not yet fully revealed but knowing that God's plan is so much better than what I can see or could try to plan on my own. In the winter I must relearn how to know He is with me, even in the struggles and the trials.

A Time to Uproot

I remember when my eldest child was a newborn, a lot of people told me to cherish every minute because he would grow up so quickly. Well, in that season of my life, as much as I tried to, I actually found it hard to do. I longed for him to crawl, walk, talk and even start school. It was much easier to do though when my second and third children were born, because I had a different perspective by then.

As I shared earlier, when we first arrived in Thailand, all of us found many aspects of moving extremely difficult. There were so many logistical things to work out and we had no idea how our children would cope emotionally minute-by-minute, not to mention day-to-day. Then, after only six months of living in Thailand, we needed to take an unplanned trip back to Australia. Dave had been trying to oversee his family's business from afar (as well as work at ZOE full-time) but the arrangement with a newly-appointed manager did not seem to be going as smoothly as anticipated. We needed to go back and decide what action to take. A one-week trip turned into a one-month long ordeal but, in God's timing, the business sold — literally as we landed back on Thai soil!

Initially, as we began to settle the children *again* into our new home in Thailand, I felt like we were finally starting a new season. We had a little bit more perspective the second-time-round on what to expect. Soon enough though, the reality of another upcoming transition started to weigh me down. We knew when we moved into our first house that it was only a short-term option. The rent was more than we wanted to pay and the house was too big for what we needed. As the lease on our house neared an end, we also needed to move the children from the preschool where they had been attending. As well, ZOE's new building project was completed so the Children's Home and offices were also relocating to a different area, much further away (all big changes in and of themselves let alone in the space of one or two months of each other).

Desperate to make this new country feel like it was our 'home,' we felt confronted with uncertainty at every turn. Where would we live? Where would our children go to school? Would the kids and I still be able to visit ZOE as often? Could we still manage with just one car? After six months of trying to become familiar with our new surroundings, the progress had already been slow but with the additional changes ahead, the 'settling in' process felt like taking two steps forward and one-and-a-half steps back.

I reflected on the contrast in my own life. When I was growing up, I lived in the same house from the time I was born until I was nineteen years old. In the subsequent nineteen years of my life, 'home' for me changed frequently. Our kids were in their ninth home, not including all the temporary homes we've stayed in on our annual trips back to Australia.

Growing up, home for me was in the suburb of Ferntree Gully or 'The Gully' as the locals called it. Ferntree Gully is in the state of Victoria, located at the foothills of the Dandenong Ranges, which was well known for the Kokoda Trail (a 1,000 step memorial walk dedicated to the Kokoda Track of WW2). Around our sixth birthdays, my dad would pack breakfast and take each one of us kids on a hike up the 1,000 steps to the One Tree Hill lookout in the national park. Our house had a huge tree in the front yard that I would climb regularly and sit up high looking down on people walking up and down the street; unaware that they were being watched by a curious girl perched on a branch. Our driveway metamorphosed into racetracks, roller-skating rinks, bicycle paths, a basketball court or whatever else our imaginations conjured up. At one end of our street was a milk bar, which served my siblings and me twenty cents worth of mixed lollies (candies) in a little white paper bag. The other direction led to a huge hill, which was fun to ride our bikes down, but not so much fun to walk up on the way to school in our foundational years.

I knew the streets around our family's home well and I walked them often. There was so much familiarity, that as I reflect, I can still picture the local fish'n'chip shop where we would sometimes get take-away dinner for a special treat on the weekend. Or the bakery where we would be sent to buy the 'baker's dozen' of white knot rolls for lunch after church. The old cemetery (established in 1873), the local swimming pool where I spent hours swimming laps as a teenager and Straub's Garage. Straub helped me find my first car and let me pay it off each time I got my paycheck from my part-time job. Those streets were some of the first places that I went as a small child, tagging along with my mum to do banking, buy groceries, post letters, pay bills or catch the train.

Fast forward to 2010, seven houses later, in a different part of the world, I found myself uncertain and longing for the familiar once again, or at least a sense of 'home' for my own children. Growing up, my home had been so stable and secure. I questioned whether my children would ever experience that. I prayed that they would.

In her book, *The Gifts of Imperfection,* Brene Brown talks about finding "the courage to believe in what we cannot see and the strength to let go of our fear of uncertainty." As I was reflecting during this season, the picture that came to my mind was one of outstretched hands. So much of what is precious to me, I naturally tend to hold tight, gripping it with firmly clasped hands, attempting to control and protect. But through these winter months I have been reminded that nothing is mine to hold *that* tightly. I continually need the strength to surrender. It is only with open hands, trusting in God and seeking His best plan, that I have truly been able to experience freedom in this area of my life.

In the winter seasons, my capacity to endure uncertainty increases as my desire to control and rely on my own strength decreases.

A Time to Heal

Ideally, the best time to repair a hole in the roof is when the sun is shining. Right? How often do we find ourselves having to try to fix things though after it's already started raining? Throughout the winter, if we can take time to slow down and really identify what needs mending, it can be a time of refreshment, healing and restoration. There's a saying, "Broken things can become blessed things if you let God do the mending."

As the lease on our first house in Thailand crept closer to its end date, we started to feel the increasing pressure to find somewhere else to live. We knew the area we wanted to move to. It was close to where some of our other missionary friends were, as well as a school that we liked. So, one day we prayed about it and decided to get in our car and drive to the spot where we wanted our next home to be. In a miraculous way that we were not expecting, we sat in our car staring out the window at a 'For Rent' sign on a house that looked like an amazing option and was within walking distance of the school. We called the phone number listed and the landlord spoke English so we arranged a look through and literally, just like that, God went before us and made a way for us to rent the house. No searching around. No stress. What a quick answer to prayer!

We all really loved living in this house. After the furniture was in place, I set to work quickly adding the finishing touches of hanging photographs and placing objects of meaning around and finally, in August 2010, we started to feel like we had a proper 'home' again. We made many wonderful memories in that house, from numerous children's parties, water fights, friends popping in, family and friends staying with us, and owning various small pets (including some cute baby turtles) but looking back, there was also no shortage of challenges.

One ordinary Thursday night, in March 2011, a magnitude 6.8 earthquake struck eastern Myanmar, near the border with Thailand and Laos. I remember I was typing on my computer when suddenly I started to feel like I was experiencing vertigo. I looked up to see the pictures and framed family photographs on the wall swaying and as I got up to walk, I had to steady myself. I met Dave on the stairs as he experienced the shakes too but neither one of us could remember what we were meant to do. Thankfully it passed quickly and our kids slept right through, unaware.

On another occasion in that house, I remember we were entertaining some friends on a Saturday afternoon. The six children were all playing nicely and so the four of us adults sat down with a coffee to catch up on each other's lives. It began raining heavily outside, which was not unusual, but then suddenly the power went out (which is also not unusual). As it was such a hot day, we laughed it off as we all sat around sweating with not even a fan to circulate the air in the lounge room. Due to the downpour, the children had all come inside too ... so ten people in one room on a hot afternoon ... you get the picture! It was not until later though, after our friends had gone home and the power finally came back on, that we realised that *not all* the power had returned to our house. Throughout that evening and then next morning we began to notice the extent of the problem we were faced with ... power points not working, fridge not working, air conditioner, fan, washing machine, air purifier, phone charger, printer ... all NOT working. Funnily enough, I like to thank God's sense of humour for this; our coffee machine and home computer were both spared! Incredibly the power board that our home computer was plugged into had a circuit breaker and whilst the power board no longer worked, it did save our computer.

Our landlord organised several electricians to come and begin surveying the damage. They spread out, soldering circuit boards on the floor in our lounge room and by the end of the day we had both air-conditioning and a refrigerator that worked (minus all the food we'd lost). Our fan needed to be taken away for repair, as well as our washing machine, air purifier and printer.

The following Tuesday night, it began raining again — and AGAIN the power went out! Dave called our landlord to explain what was happening, because we started to realise that not everyone's power was going out every time it rained — just ours. The landlord told Dave to flick the switch on the fuse board but as he did, my laptop's power-cord, which was plugged into my laptop blew up — yep, like it actually exploded! We went and checked a few other things and realised that we'd lost the use of some of the other power points, and that the refrigerator had gone off again ... this time though, thankfully it still worked when we plugged it into a different point. By Wednesday, the electricians were back again and they *seemed* to have fixed the power points again. We did have to buy new power-boards with circuit breakers for the computers though, I had to get a new power cord and we had to wait for all the other items to be fixed.

Houses in Thailand do not commonly have basements but this house did. It was a great place for storing things: baby items no longer needed, Christmas decorations, Dave's tools, his guitar ... you get the idea, oh and, sometimes even our guests. It seemed like a good space for guests to sleep when they stayed. Well, I should say, it *had been* a good place to store things and to sleep guests until the next challenge we had in that house.

One dull and dreary Saturday we drove home in some particularly heavy rain and unlike the usual downpours here, it looked like it would never stop ... it rained and rained and rained. Dave and I had sat up in the kids' bedroom for a while until they fell asleep because not only was the rain very loud, but there was also very loud thunder and flashes of lightning, plus on top of that, the power went out AGAIN!

Shortly after the children had all fallen asleep, I headed to the kitchen to get something when I was confronted by a really strange smell. I wondered what it could be so I started to walk down the stairs to the basement, then I saw it ... a huge flood of ankle-deep water! Spare mattresses literally floating around, our friend's desks that we were storing until they moved house sitting in water and cardboard storage boxes soggy and falling apart. "*Help!*" I called out.

Dave and I worked quickly together to move everything we could either upstairs or outside, and eventually collapsed in bed exhausted just after midnight. We called one of our friends, who lived about a five-minute drive away, to see if he could come and help lift some of the heavier items but it turned out he wasn't even able to leave his house due to the depth of the water in his street.

The following morning our landlord sent around someone to pump all the water out of the basement so that we were all able to go down with our mops and buckets to finish soaking up the last bit of the water. Thankfully only a few things were beyond saving. The clean-up slowly progressed and we found different spots around the house to store things. Despite the inconvenience and the mess, we were so grateful that this happened when it did. We imagined if it had occurred while we were back in Australia or while we had guests sleeping there. When we first moved in, we actually had our study area set up down in the basement but we decided to move it due to the humidity down there. So once again, our computer had been spared.

Also in 2011, the Disaster Department reported that 188 people had been killed and three others remained missing as a result of the tropical storms, which hit Thailand in late July. Floods, mudslides and heavy rain affected nearly two million people.

The Ping River (Mac Nam Ping ... meaning mother/water) joins with several other rivers to form the Chao Phraya River which then flows through the heart of Bangkok. It was up and down this passage of water that people had travelled between north and south of Thailand for hundreds of years. Interestingly, Daniel McGilvery, the first missionary to the north, took three months to arrive in Chiang Mai from Bangkok on the Ping River in 1867 *(Citylife,* Feb. 1, 2018).

During the 2011 floods, the heavy rain caused the Ping River to burst its banks and overflow into the railway station and central business district, forcing a temporary shutdown in train services to northern Thailand. Whilst out and about during this time, we were redirected many times due to road closures. It was reported that over one hundred highways and roads nationwide were impassable. By October, extensive flooding in Bangkok, and uncertainty about how long the problem would remain, resulted in many shelves in the supermarkets becoming empty. In some stores, like 7Eleven, there wasn't even bottled water left for sale. Other dried foods, oil and canned goods were also scarce. This was due to a disruption in the supply chain as many of the major factories were under water and parts of Bangkok were shut down for the whole month.

During our time in that house, we experienced a lot of heavy rain. I could share many other stories about times when our house flooded, or even when school closed due to the flooding. Like another time, in the middle of one big downpour, we decided to head out in our car to see how everyone else in our neighbourhood was coping with the rising water levels.

There were a few roads near us that we couldn't drive through but what was great was that this particular day, just as the rain started to lessen, out came the most beautiful double rainbow. As we gasped and "ooohhhhed" and "ahhhhed" at how wonderfully colourful it was in the sky, our three little ones broke out into song, "I can sing a rainbow ... " and it reminded me a lot of our journey here. The very 'rain' that took us out of our comfort zone, that soaked us with heartache, homesickness and so many other challenges also brought us the blessings of a clear and beautiful rainbow in the sky. As I reflected on the projects going on at ZOE, the smiling faces of the rescued children and the promises of a better future with a hope in God, I was reminded again that God is the same yesterday, today and forever. We can trust His faithfulness to mend that which has been broken, and we can be assured that as we look up to Him after the heaviest of downpours; there will be a rainbow — a reminder of His promises, right there in the sky.

A Time to Slow Down

I used to feel like I was always saying to my children, "Hurry up!" "Quick ... " "Come on!" "Can you go a little bit faster, please?" But one thing about living here, that's in stark contrast to me always trying to rush everything, is the very relaxed Thai culture. One morning, David and I had set the alarm for 1.00 a.m. And by 2.00 a.m. we had snuggled the kids into the car with their blankets and favourite soft toys and were headed for Ban Maesa village, four or so hours' drive away.

When I was a child, I always thought it was so much fun leaving to go somewhere in the middle of the night, or early morning before the sun had risen. To me, it always seems to add a sense of mystery and excitement to the journey. This particular morning, we were on our way to celebrate the wedding of some friends — our first time to a village wedding and for our children, their first big trip to a village.

Jip and Jack, who both worked at ZOE, were due to be married at 7:30 a.m. on a Saturday morning. With the odds stacked against us: me getting carsick on the long, winding journey and our youngest child being feverish (we later found out he had a nasty ear infection), we finally arrived at the village just after 6:00 a.m. We were greeted by one of the ZOE parents, a lady who had lived in this village before working at ZOE. She still had a house there that her mother took care of. Seated around a fire pit (in the middle of the stilt house) we sat warming up and sipping hot drinks. It was hard to believe that there was a wedding beginning in less than two hours because the mood was so relaxed and there was such a 'calm' atmosphere.

It was soon announced that the wedding would not be starting till 8am after all, which added an extra element of 'no need to rush' and made things even more relaxed. As we took the time to explore and walk around the beautiful village, the word passed around that the wedding would now begin at 8:30am And then it changed to 9:00 a.m. Did anybody seem stressed? No, not one bit!

Eventually, sometime after 8:00 a.m., a bell could be heard ringing and a friend explained, "Gin khaow." We knew those words well. It was time to eat (literally 'eat rice'). We made our way to Jip's house where we were ushered into the living room. Sitting on the floor around a generous serving of rice, curries, vegetables and soup; we ate and enjoyed the company of those around us. Actually, I should explain that those around us were mainly just the few other foreigners who had come to the wedding — our friends, the Tang family and Mike (CEO of ZOE who was the one performing the marriage ceremony). What was amusing though was that the villagers, who were eating outside, kept looking in on us through the doors as we ate and bringing in more and more food. Our children, the only 'white' ones present in the whole village, drew a lot of stares. I even had little children looking at me during the wedding ceremony and pointing to my eyes with amazement. I guessed blue eyes weren't seen around those parts very often.

From Jip's house we walked up a steep road that led to the village church. I had to keep reminding myself that I was going to a wedding. No one was stressed, no one was rushing and I was beginning to understand how this uncomplicated, relaxed way of life could actually ... be ... uh ... better!

I heard a foreigner ask a local person one day if it was rude to walk around eating. The man looked confused asking, "Why would anyone need to?" Sometimes in our Western culture we get busy and eat on the run — breakfast in the car on the way to work, lunch on the way to the next meeting. Sometimes we lose that sense of the value of just sitting and being, enjoying food, valuing the company and actually taking time to share meals together.

So, in the winter, my challenge from all of this was to simply slow down. To sit and eat without rushing off. To enjoy other people's company. To stop striving, planning and overthinking everything. To just allow myself to 'be' ... to see afresh, to notice what was going on around me and for goodness sakes — to try not to always overcomplicate things.

A Time to Give Up

As I have mentioned, when I have chosen to open up my hands and surrender issues, I have begun to see how much better God is at looking after the precious areas of my life than I am. Yes! Who would have known? He's *much* more able than I am. I'll be honest though — it hasn't been easy. There have been some rough times over the years where I have felt totally unsure of what to do and what direction to take. It has been during these times that I have had to consciously stop myself from curling up my fingers that so desperately want to take control and my hands that want to grip tight and cradle closely whatever it is in there at that time.

Throughout the winters, I feel like God asks me (again and again) to release my cares, my family, my friendships, my plans, my reputation, my insecurities and my hopes to Him.

When I am able to do this, I can truthfully say that He does not let me down. He has never failed me. When I have been able to release something to Him, being deliberate to flatten my palm and outstretch my arm to Him, He has always come through. Maybe it hasn't been how I'd thought He would. Maybe it hasn't been in my timing. Maybe it wasn't even the way I would've liked but I know — and trust — that ultimately, He knows best.

One day I was smiling to myself and praising God while doing my ironing. An issue with a friend that I had needed to surrender and hold loosely in order to let God come in and work had now, suddenly, turned itself around. What I had been so unsure about, I had quietly opened up to God to work out. It was several months later that I started to feel close to this person once again realising that indeed, God had gone before me and protected that friendship. Had I taken the route of holding on too tight or speaking out of line in defense, I know that it could've been a very different story. Sometimes these situations are so hard to hold loosely but, in my experience, it's totally worth it. Usually, we have no idea what God is doing 'behind the scenes' on our behalf.

A Time to Tear Down

Most people are familiar with the wooden game Jenga. The one where you start with a stack of blocks and then the players take it in turns to start removing them one-by-one hoping that, on their turn, the tower doesn't fall down.

In February 2018, Dave was sharing a word-picture of how his life had felt like a Jenga tower. He'd been the one building it carefully, stacking it up, making sure that everything appeared okay, it was solid and 'in place.' Upon reflection, everything did 'look right' until about mid-2017. At the beginning of the year the part of the game (where blocks start being removed one-by-one) began. Looking back, there were wobbles and swaying throughout the first half of the year but by midyear, the tower had inevitably come crashing down with a mighty thud. After the shock and disbelief, all that remained was a stack of blocks in a messy pile.

Sometimes piles of blocks can teach us things though, and that was how it was in the time that followed the falling tower — a season of *many* lessons.

As the weeks turned into months ... tears represented healing at work ... confusion transformed into a deeper understanding and ever so slowly, the mess became a time for regrouping and seeing things from a different perspective.

Just like a cold winter feels like it will never end, so too did that season of the fallen tower. But then, out of nowhere one day came a gentle breeze — just slightly warmer than the day before, a glimmer of sunshine and a tiny new flower-bud to admire. And just like how spring follows winter, so it was after the season of 'winter' in my husband's life.

One of the things we both learnt quickly in this winter-time, was that if Dave's tower was to be built the same way again, another collapse would most likely occur. Just like in the real game, the falling tower could potentially keep happening over and over. So going forward, we knew the tower must be rebuilt in a *new* way. This posed the question, that if the tower needed to be built differently, then how?

So often in our lives when God wants to remold us and make something ncw, there is a period of time where we must let go of old ways and relearn His way. We must submit again to His authority, humbling ourselves like clay in the potter's hands. We take our messy pile of blocks and ask, "Please make me into something new!" This, of course, is rarely an enjoyable experience. As someone who has never had particularly flexible muscles, I think of it like being stretched. When our muscles are tight and we stretch, it is so painful. Many weeks later, after going through pain day after day, we start to notice how the muscle we have been stretching is slowly becoming stronger and more pliable. It can be used, and relied upon, in different ways.

When playing Jenga, have you noticed how people play variations of the game? One alternative being that there are words written on the blocks and when you remove a block, you must read, and do, what it says. During the season of 'the falling tower,' Dave had to learn all about what made his tower fall. He had to go back and examine each block, identifying all the pieces that made up his life. Looking at each block on its own, he had to surrender each one to God as if to say, "Do you want this one?" As each block was looked at carefully, a sorting process took place. Some blocks were still needed and some were not. Understandably, some blocks were easier to let go of than others.

The 'new' tower is a continual work in progress. It's not finished yet but God is in the process of working on it — sometimes more slowly than Dave may like. I know though that it's being built in His perfect timing. The tower doesn't look anything like the one before it did, and that's okay, in fact, it's better. Whenever God is sitting in the driver's seat, it's always better.

Ironically right after David shared his word-picture of the Jenga tower, we had just finished a counselling session. As we walked into the reception area, there (on a little table, set up for children) stood a bright Jenga tower. I quickly grabbed my phone and took a photo of it to remember that moment in time — thankful that God had left us a reminder of the season of the falling tower and His promise of making something new.

A Time to Be Still

You know, sometimes there are stories that can only be shared after a certain period of time has elapsed and some healing has occurred.

This is one of them!

"Ladies and Gentlemen, this is your captain speaking. It looks like we've hit some unexpected turbulence and I'm going to turn on the seatbelt sign. The seatbelt sign is now on. Please remain seated until the seatbelt sign goes off. Thank you."

As someone who has struggled with motion sickness her *whole* life, these types of announcements make me instantly break out in a cold sweat. On our last day in Australia in 2017, I had intentionally reduced my caffeine intake, sipped water all day, eaten healthy food, taken my travel sickness medication and of course prayed; but then as the plane made its way into the air ... the dreaded 'turbulence' announcement rang through the cabin loud and clear.

I decided to avoid the tray they were bringing around for dinner but even still, the combination of the food smells and onset of unsteady movement in the plane was enough to set me off on a path of a VERY-MISERABLE-JOURNEY back to Thailand.

After about five hours of continuous vomiting, I staggered unsteadily off the first flight, spare sick bags tucked into my pockets. It was as we departed the plane though, that the unexpected occurred, our youngest shrieked a panicked cry — he too was feeling sick. We grabbed a spare bag and, not losing pace with the rest of the passengers departing the flight, we held it for him as we all kept walking and he lost the contents of his last meal. Poor guy.

At the airport in between flights, all I could do was to be still. I was weak and every part of my body ached. Finding a spot on the floor, I lay down, exhausted and drifted in and out of a state of dehydrated, distressed sleep.

Waiting till the last minute, my family gently guided me to the next flight but I already had a terrible feeling that this one was not going to be much different to the last. But I was wrong ... IT WAS SO MUCH WORSE! Not only was *I* sick for the whole flight, but so were TWO of my children! Poor Dave! He lost count of how many times he had to go and ask for more bags.

Just when we thought we would be stuck in the air feeling nauseated forever, we finally touched down and stumbled weakly off the plane. Lacking strength and energy we tried to focus on the fact that we were almost home. Making our way through immigration and baggage, we exited the airport and found a songthaew* to drive us the twenty-minute or so ride home. Through the winding streets and familiar city sites, we all stared unemotionally out the back of the truck until we were eventually dropped at the front of our house.

> * A covered ute/pickup truck with two rows of seats in the back —
> 'songthaew' literally means 'two rows'.

As we unlocked the front gate and started to haul the suitcases to the door one-by-one, there it was ... the final, depressing, reminder of what had been a terrible, horrible, no good, very bad day. Our youngest threw up all over the front doorstep. Yep! We'd made it home.

But, as you know, 'turbulence' doesn't *just* strike on planes. The winter seasons have definitely included some turbulent times for our family. Unsteadiness, uncertainty and a bumpy ride have jolted and stretched us in ways that we have not experienced before. And there have been days when the words 'BE STILL' in the command, "Be still and know that I am God" have gripped me in the same way like at the airport that day when I literally *had* to be still.

That day, I needed to be 'physically' still, to block out all the other noises and movement and activity around me. But sometimes the noises and the distractions around us are people's comments, the enemy's lies, our own insecurities, negative thoughts or unmet expectations. Sometimes activities are distractions like when we lack boundaries, overcommit or choose not to let go of our control. In the end, it's all the same. We must eventually be still.

Being still is a bit like saying, I will not pay attention to ... or focus my eyes on the storm swirling around me but I will trust in you God. *Being still* cannot be done in front of a computer screen, on our phone or in the crowded places of our lives. If we will not *be still* voluntarily, then sometimes it will take a big shaky dose of turbulence to get our attention and have us crawling into a still, small, quiet place alone to understand and know, HE is God — not us.

Whilst doing a six-week study at our church and in our small groups on a book called 'God's Grand Story,' I was telling a friend about my journaling. After finishing our chapters on Moses and the Israelites, I had written, *"I hope that through our family's wilderness experiences that we really truly learn the lessons that God would have us learn. That we would not miss the 'Promised Land' of what God has for us next and that we would grow in our trust and obedience to Him."* How challenging to think that no matter whether God answers our prayers in the way we want him to or not, that we would fully trust in Him. In this season, we must make time to *BE STILL* through the turbulence, storms and thunder. Really still.

A Time to Stay Close

Have you ever had a year that was so great you thought it would be hard to ever top it? Where success and prosperity flowed abundantly in every area. Or maybe there was a year that you were glad to see finally finished (like 2020 with the covid pandemic). Maybe that year had felt like a deep dark cave with dangerous twists and turns, slippery surfaces, damp musty smells and little-to-no light to guide your path. Or like the falling tower experience that my husband had, where his whole world felt like it had come crashing down.

A few years ago, our family went on a mini road trip to the Chiang Dao Caves. After proceeding into the caves, we were faced with a decision. There was a short track with open spaces and lighting that meant people could easily walk along unassisted, or a more adventurous path that involved exploring an unlit part of the caves and a much longer trek. We would have to hire a guide, carrying an old-fashioned kerosene lantern to go with us on the more dangerous path, but we were all keen for an adventure so we picked the harder option and set off excitedly.

The kids enthusiastically followed right along behind the guide, whereas I ended up at the back of the group, trying to capture memories and take pictures on my phone. What I soon realised though was that the further I lingered behind, the less I could see. Each time I stopped and tried to take a photo, the light from the lantern would disappear and I was left in complete darkness. As I attempted to catch up with everyone else, I stumbled and strained to see where to put my feet and where to duck my head down and not hit a stalactite, but it was extremely difficult outside of the circumference of the lantern's light. Pretty soon, I learnt that I had to stay close by the guide and in the light for my own safety.

I couldn't help but reflect, as I stumbled along at the back, at how much this cave experience was also a lot like life. I was reminded of one of the first Bible verses that I had learnt as a child. Psalm 119:105, "Your word is a lamp to my feet and a light to my path." Inside the cave, without the lamp for our feet and the light for the path, we would've been in a lot of danger — danger of slipping, falling down a hole, hitting our heads or going the wrong way.

In life, there are not only our own personal times of darkness, but there are also worrying world-events that can leave us gripped with fear. When I hear certain news reports, I often wish I hadn't. They are just so devastating and sad. How can humans treat each other with such hate and evil intentions? If we just sat and listened to the news all day, I'm sure there would be feelings of hopelessness that would hang over us, dark clouds of despair. But if we meditate on God's word and really put our trust in Him, we see Him as the light — all that is good and perfect and real love. To keep ourselves from being caught up in the world's despair and devastated by hopelessness, we need to stay close to the source of light, transformed by His promises. We can find hope ... even in the darkness. We must draw near to the source; stay close by the light and remember that He walks with us.

In the seasons of darkness and during our striving to find God, may we understand that 'THE LIGHT' is there for our benefit, our safety and to give us hope. May we not be too self-sufficient so that we forget our need for 'THE LIGHT' or walk with too much distance from it. In the wintery seasons it can be hard to keep on the right track, but as we grip onto the promises of God, the Holy Spirit helps us to endure — sticking to the course and not being easily distracted by other things that would draw us away from 'THE LIGHT'. My prayer is that I would also reflect the light, the peace and the hope in me wherever God places me in the world. Despite being in a season of winter, may I still reflect light to all those around me who so desperately need it.

A Time to Build

When I was growing up, my family had an open fireplace, so learning how to build a fire to keep the room warm was all part of living in our home — collecting twigs and smaller logs, learning how to gradually add larger logs and keep the fire alive.

One winter, whilst visiting Australia, we were blessed to be able to stay in a little cottage with a potbelly fireplace. I loved seeing all three of my children also creating memories — collecting kindling, carrying big logs and learning how to start a fire. In 2009 when we heard about ZOE for the first time, something definitely 'sparked' in us. And a bit like a fire, we, hypothetically, started down a path of collecting kindling, blowing the small sparks of the fire, fueling it as it grew and tending it, waiting and watching to see what would happen until ... eventually all these years later, we are at a stage where it looks like there are starting to be some deep burning coals.

One night during our stay in the little cottage, Dave was due to be leaving because he was sharing at a young adults' group that night. Since it was so cold, he tried to light a fire for us before he left. It really didn't take off though, and he had to leave before there was anything but a few small flickers. After putting the children to bed, I began to try ... actually I had several tries but, for some reason, I couldn't get it to start. I huffed and I puffed ... and I nearly blew the house down trying all my old tricks; but it was not until about ten o'clock that I could honestly say there was finally a 'good' fire that looked like it would give off some decent heat. Eventually, once it got going, it was hot and fierce ... unquenchable you might say.

There's a quote, "*A mighty flame follows a tiny spark.*" *

* Dante Alighieri was an Italian poet and writer who is best known for his epic poem "The Divine Comedy.

Sometimes our little sparks seem like they'll never come to be much. They may fizzle for a while and then die out. They may burn quickly like paper and then just as quickly turn to ash. I was reminded though how sometimes these small sparks catch onto something that starts another spark and then that spark starts another ... pretty soon there are small fires burning all over the place. What ended up being interesting about this particular trip to Australia, was how we also started to notice small sparks of interest and offers by other people to help us. God was in these little sparks that were being lit. We noticed new and fresh passion in people who wanted to share about ZOE's work with their friends and colleagues.

Since that trip, our little team in Australia started to grow and we now have some trusted people in our circle who help us with various tasks. What's more though, is that they have a burning desire to stop trafficking and to make a difference in the lives of children. Just like that quote, we look forward to the day (actually we can't wait) when the mighty flame follows these tiny sparks.

A Time to Plant

Have you ever been really focused on working hard on a particular area of your life, but just not seen the rewards for all your effort as quickly as you expected to? It can be very discouraging when you try to do what's right and nothing happens. It could be at work, a hobby or at home in your family. The Chinese bamboo tree first spoke to me when we moved into the Transitional Home. It was a point in time where we were trying to build our language and understand culture. It was about the five-year mark of our time in Thailand and it felt like things were taking much longer than expected to come to fruition.

I think a lot of us struggle with patience, don't we? We live in a world where we don't like to wait. It's a world of instant information, instant messaging, instant everything — we can easily fall into the trap of coming to expect 'life' and relationships will build quickly too. We want to see immediate results, but a good lesson on this subject is the story of the Chinese Bamboo Tree. It seems that when this tree is planted, watered, and nurtured for an entire growing season it doesn't outwardly grow — not even a centimeter. There are no visible signs of growth, in spite of providing all of the things that plants need to grow.

Then, after the second growing season, a season in which the farmer takes extra care to water, fertilise and care for the bamboo tree, the tree still doesn't sprout. Nothing! And so it goes as the sun rises and sets for another four solid years. Nothing! The farmer has nothing tangible to show for all of his labour trying to grow the tree.

For us, all these years passed when our patience was tested, and we began to wonder if our efforts caring for and watering the 'trees' in our life would ever be rewarded. It's easy to let doubt set in and question the value of your efforts in these moments and hard to resist the urge to quit.

Then, along comes the fifth year. In this year the Chinese bamboo tree seed finally sprouts but not only that, it grows up to 27 metres tall in only six weeks! Had the farmer dug up his little seed every year to see if it was growing, he would have stunted the tree's growth. In other words, the actions caused by self-doubt would stop or slow down the eventual growth of the tree. In seasons of planting, we need faith and hope in the things not yet seen. It takes a lot of faith to wait and not be afraid. Questions like, "But what if it never...?" start to creep in. It takes belief to keep going. It takes confidence to trust.

Sometimes it takes years of loving someone or something with no response or results. During those first few years of 'life,' very little visible growth can be seen because all of the work and the growth is focused on creating a deep and diverse root system. But when that metaphorical 'tree' grows, a miracle takes place. I encourage you with whatever you face in the winter, keep loving and tending ... the miracle is on its way.

So many people in the Bible had long waits before their miracles came: Joseph, Noah, David. Again, we are reminded that our timing is not God's timing. God is with us in the waiting, and He is not just concerned about the outcome, but also the journey. In the winter we learn to be patient. We learn to keep watering. And we live with expectation that a miracle will come.

Just before we moved house in October 2018, the landlord took us through each room inside as well as outdoors, explaining everything he thought we might need to know. Upon seeing a huge tree, propped up and hovering over the driveway (and dropping lots of leaves) we asked him what type of tree it was. He replied that it was a mango tree and added that he thought it bore fruit for many months of the year. To say that we were excited at the thought of having an abundance of juicy, sweet mangoes was an understatement!

In the months that followed, as we swept those piles of falling leaves each day, we waited expectantly for the tree's first sign of fruit. Month after month we waited. Until May, when we suddenly started to spot them, high up on the branches, far from our reach. A few mangoes did eventually fall from the tree but, when they did, they were over-ripe or had evidence that a squirrel or two had already sampled them.

My husband, not to be outdone by the squirrels, climbed up onto the carport roof with a makeshift, net-fruit-picker and recruited the rest of us to be 'catchers' down below. Waiting on the ground to seize the mangoes as they catapulted through the air, we filled our buckets and baskets to overflowing. The warm temperature inside our house was the perfect climate to ripen the mangoes and 1-2 days after picking, they reached ... perfection! We ate mango after mango. Gave away mangoes and had enough to cut up and freeze as well.

The same week we hit the 'mango jackpot,' my daughter discovered that the papaya tree in the backyard also had fruit ready to pick. So, she decided to start making *som-tum* (green papaya salad). She'd learnt how to make it at school and generously kept offering it at mealtimes for our family. We enjoyed eating as much as she would make us. It was so delicious. One night after filling up on *som-tum* and our homegrown mangoes, I sent a message to a friend with a food photo saying: *"I never thought it would feel so good to be eating the food off our land!* 😎 *It makes me want to plant more trees!"*

Then after I'd sent the message, it hit me. The sudden realisation that here I was, relishing in the juicy fruits of two trees that I didn't plant, nor had I watered when they were just sprouts in the ground, or pruned as saplings. In fact, I hadn't done any 'work' at all, well ... except for sweeping up all those leaves! Suddenly I began to wonder how many years ago those trees had been planted. Who had cared for them all this time? Who had helped them grow to maturity and strength, able to produce fruit and withstand the various weather elements? And whilst I will probably never find out the answers to those questions, I suddenly saw a connection between that mango tree and prayer. Hear me out! Sometimes we pray for people, for healing, or (in the world's view) impossible situations to turn around, but we don't see the answer until much, much later. Have you ever prayed about something but it took years until you saw the answer come to be?

So just like my family and I were enjoying the fruit from a tree that we didn't plant or care for, I realised that I was eating and enjoying the fruit of other people's 'answered prayers' every day ... okay that sounds weird! What I mean is, my life is a testimony to many answered prayers by my grandparents, my parents, churches in Australia and our friends. So, if prayer is like planting a seed, then continuing to pray is like watering it and receiving the answer is like eating the fruit.

When it comes to big prayers like rescuing children from child trafficking or ending modern day slavery, although we hope to, we might never actually see the answers to these things in our lifetime; but we can be the ones planting the tiny seeds. Let's continue to plant seeds and pray big ... expectant prayers ... whether we get to see the end result, or not.

A Time to Hope

Nature continues to quietly remind me about the simplistic and profound way that God works through our day-to-day. Small faithful actions can bring life and beauty back to places that once seemed void of hope. I love the word 'hope.' You only need the smallest little bit to cling to, and you have it. Hope is what individuals, groups, nations and the world all need. It's so powerful. It's life-giving. It's transformative.

We have this small, tiled area out the back of our house with basically just enough space for our washing machine and some baskets. On one side of the tiled perimeter is about a foot-wide strip of rocks. In February 2019, Dave decided to transplant some shrubs from the front of the house to this rocky spot out the back. Unlike a surgeon who specialises in moving organs from one person's body to another, or even a gardener who understands how to care for plants' roots properly, as they're moved to a new home; Dave and I are both unskilled and unqualified in the garden. So, in situations like this, all we really had was *hope* that our transplanted foliage would take to its new environment and not die.

Every day we set about watering. At first all seemed fine, but then we started to notice that the plants were looking really sad and their leaves began changing from green to brown. We both thought the transplant had most likely failed, which was not surprising, but something prompted us to continue faithfully watering — expecting the best.

This went on for several months when one day, I was out the back doing the usual routine, putting on a load of washing and watering the plants, when I noticed something new ... a tiny sprout! A little shoot protruding from the ground! Life! I also noticed that the leaves, which had previously looked like they were dying, had some colour returning to them. Finally, we had a sign that they *might* actually survive.

We see this sort of thing a lot here too with people. Missionaries arrive to work on the field, students transfer from different schools, newcomers show up at churches recently relocated by their organisations. It's a similar cycle. We can even see it in our own families as our children, or our spouse, endure difficult seasons, trials, injuries or adjustments.

Sometimes when people experience dramatic change, they may initially appear to cope quite well. They may have seemingly adapted to their current environment, until suddenly they reach the stage where the 'newness' of the situation starts to wear thin and the telltale signs of the struggle begin. All of a sudden, they seem sad, homesick, frustrated, angry or cynical. What once had 'life' begins to fade into dried out desperation — a thirst for what they left behind and the familiar once again. Metaphorically speaking their leaves start to wither and turn brown and the previously green stem appears droopy. As a community, a friend, or a parent our job is simply to water and wait. We can encourage, we can sympathise, and we can assure them that things will improve. We can surely remember a similar time ... we've been there too.

All through the months of the painful struggle, we trust and believe that God is working through this process, just as He has worked through ours. Even though no one can see what's happening below the surface, deep in the ground and around the roots, He does. He knows how to bring life to the deep and dark places. Harsh conditions and dry spirits do not turn Him away. Our role is to faithfully water, hoping and trusting for that evidence seen in a tiny sprout. Faithfulness is what we can give in the everyday, mundane, ordinary choices that we make to serve, to smile, to encourage and to hope alongside those who just need the smallest piece to grasp on to.

Often the habit of faithfully watering goes unnoticed. It's easy to forget or turn a blind eye, especially when there are 'better' things to do. How often the tasks, which bring praise and recognition, seem so much more appealing than the dreary habits formed when nobody else is around. But it is these small, often unnoticed choices each day, that we see are actually the ones which became the most important decisions we ever made.

As we sit with those whose leaves are dying and whose soil is dry and we faithfully water, we know that the One who is enough for us, is enough for them too. He who gives us hope, who brought us through, is also at work in them even when we cannot see. Even when there is no sign of new life, we must trust that His timing is not ours. And while we devotedly water — waiting and hoping, He uses the time to grow our faith and trust and to strengthen our relationship with Him. Often, just when we thought we were only being used to help someone else, we see that God is also using their life and their struggle to powerfully transform and strengthen us too.

Through all the ups and downs in the winters, I can look back now and see God's hand in every situation. My heart's desire is that my trust would grow through each winter experience, and that I would fully submit to God's will — regardless of my own.

The winter times so far have included floods, food shortages, military coups, setbacks, unsettling times, lockdown/isolation and death. As a family, we have cried, mourned, questioned and picked up broken pieces. There have been days when I have felt like I could hardly catch my breath as life's circumstances tried to pull me down below a surface of untamed waves. I have driven my car with tears streaming, unable to pray but merely letting worship songs speak deep into my soul and barely finding the words to utter, "I choose to trust."

Other days, the winter has felt like a never-ending marathon. I've questioned, why am I running? Where am I going? Who am I even running against? There have been days when I questioned how I would even put one foot in front of the other. Instead of looking up to see what was up ahead, my vision has been focused on my feet and I seemed to have temporarily lost my way. But I am reminded in these times that God is with me through both the happy experiences and the tough ones, the victories and the losses, the planned and the unplanned. My hope lies not in what I can see as I look down at my tired and weary feet, it's in the One who gives me air in my lungs, strength in my legs and His promise of never leaving me.

Some of the most powerful work happens in the silence of winter, and I am beginning to value the importance of the quiet, slow growth. I don't want to come to regret missed opportunities. I want to choose to stop instead and rest when I need to catch my breath. I want to recognise the moments that I need to look up and dream again, refocus on the road ahead and develop a new way of seeing. I don't want to miss these moments in life. And through them all, I so desperately want to confess, He is Lord. And then it happens, before I know it, spring is in the air ...

Discussion Questions

How can you honour your winter season by getting real with your schedule and making some extra time to be still, relax and rest?

Are you using the winter as a time for deep reflection and preparation? For building reserves and renewing hope? Or are you allowing yourself to become depleted?

"Just because something is hard does not mean it is not good." Can you think of a time that this has been true in your life?

What small victories can you identify in this season? Is there any guilt, discouragement or uncertainty that you need to shake off before moving on?

Some of the most powerful work happens in the silence of winter, how can you learn to value the importance of this season of quiet, slow growth?

How deep are you able to go with your friends, family and your own self-reflection at this time?

What are your deepest fears and inhibitions right now?

My kids still ask me to make this soup when they're not feeling well.

-CHICKEN & CORN SOUP-

Ingredients

- **2 cups chicken broth/stock**
- **1 can creamed corn**
- **1 tsp soy sauce**
- **1 tsp corn flour / cornstarch (mixed with a small amount of cold water)**
- **1 egg , whisked**
- **1 cup shredded cooked chicken (optional)**
- **Salt and pepper, to taste**
- **3 tbsp sliced shallots (optional)**

Sometimes my kids like to add vermicelli noodles to their soup too.

Instructions

1. Place broth, creamed corn, soy sauce and corn flour / water mixture in a saucepan over high heat.
2. Bring to boil, then turn down the heat to medium and stir occasionally. Cook for 5 minutes or until slightly thickened.
3. Adjust seasoning with salt, turn off heat, and slowly whisk in the egg so it cooks throughout the soup.
4. Add the chicken, season, and serve, garnish with shallots.

No need to wait until you feel sick to eat this soup. It's a great winter's day lunch option. Serve with crusty toast.

Don't tell anyone what's in these!

-HEALTHY BROWNIES-

Black beans are the secret ingredient in these brownies.

Ingredients
- 1 can black beans, drained and rinsed
- 3 large eggs
- 1/3 cup melted coconut oil (or ghee, or combination of both)
- 1/4 cup cocoa powder
- 1/8 tsp sea salt
- 1 tsp pure vanilla extract
- 1/4 cup honey
- 1/4 cup coconut sugar (paste not granules)
- 1/4 cup gluten-free/dairy-free chocolate chips
- 1/4 cup chopped raw nuts (optional)

Instructions
1. Preheat oven to 170°C.
2. Grease and line an 8×12 inch baking pan.
3. Place beans and coconut oil in the food processor and blend until really smooth. Add the eggs and blend again.
4. Add cocoa powder, salt, vanilla, honey and sugar and blend until smooth. (It will look runny, but don't worry.)
5. Remove the blade and gently stir in your chocolate chips and nuts, or just sprinkle the chips and nuts on top after you pour into the pan.
6. Transfer mixture to the prepared pan. Bake for 35 minutes, or until brownies are set in the center and a toothpick comes out clean.
7. Cool completely, cut into squares and enjoy!

For the longest time, I refused to tell my kids what was in these brownies. That is until they promised me that they'd still love them, even once they knew. I'll leave it up to you whether you disclose the secret ingredient or not!

Hello Spring

'God uses this season to remind us more than anything that He loves us.'

At the point when it feels like winter will never end, new life blooms into colour once again. In the physical sense, spring is the season for renewal, regrowth and new beginnings. And everything gets a little less cold and a lot more beautiful.

My grandma was known for her garden. She had the loveliest backyard I had ever seen. It was like you'd imagine an enchanted forest to be, or a scene from the Secret Garden movie. She would delight in walking people through it and explaining what everything was and giving a little story about each plant, flower or tree. As a child though, all I wanted to do was to run and play hide-and-seek with my siblings or cousins. As an adult, it would always make me smile when I would accompany her through the garden listening to her stories while my children ran and hid, just like I did as a child, squealing with the pleasure, excitement and freedom that being in her garden made us all feel. There seemed to be an endless amount of hiding places from the old garden shed, the greenhouse, behind a big old tree or right down the back near the vegetable patch. A sensory buffet amongst the sounds of birds and the tinkling of wind chimes, the combination of fragrances, shapes and variety of colours in abundance.

In the spring seasons of life, we experience new opportunities, clarity, personal growth and transformation. We may also start to recognise beauty in what was previously seen as a mess, reach acceptance where there had been a struggle and start to 'weed out' in order to make space for new growth. In the spring our hope is renewed, prayers are answered and calmness returns. We get to stop and smell the roses. Again, through this season, we are reminded to trust God's timing and not our own. It's a time to learn (or relearn) the lessons of reliance on Him and not our own understanding. It's appreciating the blessings of fruitfulness and believing that the 'pruning' takes place for our benefit and growth. It's learning to come just as we are and experience the love and acceptance of our Maker, who, more than anything, wants us to know without a doubt that He loves us!

Goodbyes

Dave was telling some new volunteers that for the first few years of living in Thailand, he kept trying to identify the rhythm, or flow of life here and eventually he realised that there wasn't one. There was no 'normal.' Living in a transient community means that all of us have had to learn to make friends quickly and say goodbye often. We've come to understand that although we don't get to see our extended family and close friends often, and that when we do, we hold them tightly and appreciate every minute that we share together. And, when we voice our goodbyes, we're never really sure when we'll get to embrace each other again.

Throughout life there are always goodbyes. Some are easy and some are hard. I remember being so happy to say goodbye to university at the completion of my four-year degree. I excitedly waved goodbye to family and friends as a newlywed, departing overseas on my honeymoon. And it's the same with winter. I am always happy to be out of the cold and into the warmer months once again. Saying goodbye to the winter seasons of my life is no different, despite the lessons learnt — I welcome the spring!

Living overseas it feels like we are always saying goodbye

to someone. Rarely a month passes when we don't. A family member going back home, a short-term team leaving, a friend returning to their country on furlough, fellow ZOE missionaries heading to America to fundraise, children from the international school going to live in another country, teachers getting job appointments on the other side of the world ... you get the idea. The lifestyle here amongst the foreigners is very temporary and just when you make that friend, it seems they go ... just like that.

On the tough days I question how our hearts are meant to handle it. Don't make friends? Be closed off? Stop inviting guests over? Just don't 'commit' or go deep in any friendships? Stay inside the house? I don't really believe any of these options are the answer. But honestly, there have been moments when I've heard the news of *another friend leaving,* and I just didn't think I had it in me to say even one more goodbye.

I remember one time when I was a young adult and I was visiting my grandma. She started sharing with me about a friend who had passed away. I don't even know why I questioned her because I sort of presumed she would've gone to the funeral, but when I brought it up, she replied that she had chosen not to go. This was an unusual response for my grandma who had a lot of friends and seemed to know almost everybody in her small town. But her words that day have never left me. She said, "I've been to so many funerals this month, I just couldn't go to another one." And now I get that, in a way. I have felt like that too. Although it's just moving country and not departing from this earthly life, sometimes I feel like I just can't cope with any more heartache.

One day, many years ago now, we had to say goodbye to two little girls who had been part of the ZOE family for a few years. The sisters had been living at ZOE since January 2010. I know because they arrived just before we did. And two of our children were the same age as them. I feel blessed that I got to see the transformations in their precious lives. I remember the first time I met the younger one. She was a quiet and lethargic toddler as a result of the way she'd been treated but by the time she left, she was a vibrant, outgoing preschooler with a zest for life. The older sister had a determined and playful personality, a real girly-girl with a sense of style and love of life. To see their happy little faces one last time as they smiled and waved from the back of the car, these two girls were going to be able to be reunited with their parents ... parents who had dramatically turned their lives around in order to regain custody of their girls, have a fresh start and be a family once again. I was happy for them ... really, I was, but even *good* goodbyes can be difficult sometimes.

The sense of what 'family' means and what 'community' is, have changed for me over the years. These concepts now extend far beyond race, culture, or traditions and I like that. I want to accept 'different' and be open to letting go of what I am accustomed to and be able to *fully live* the life that is here ... goodbyes and all. And to me, that's part of what springtime is all about. It's the beauty in the mess and the joy in the sorrow. It's about getting up after the falling down and the new growth that follows being pruned.

New Life

In March 2016, a work colleague asked me to help her with a sewing project and so we sat down to brainstorm ideas for a bag design — which needed to hold a drink bottle, notebook, pen and highlighter for an upcoming holiday program. And it needed to fit in with a 'Life is a Highway' theme. Well, if you know me, you know that I love 'a theme'! After some discussion, I suggested making the bags out of old denim jeans. I knew a secondhand shop that sold jeans, some for as little as 10 baht a pair (45 cents).

Her approval was all I needed to be off on my way, a new project to get excited about — I was one happy girl. It was only as I started sewing the jean-bags that I began to ponder about how amazing it was that an old pair of jeans, previously cast into the cheapest pile in a second-hand shop, seemingly unwanted and discarded, could actually be transformed into something totally different ... something with a new use and a new purpose. After making a practice-bag, my daughter quickly swung it over her shoulder and took it to school the next day. "Can you make all my friends one?" she asked after school. "They all really liked my bag."

With each new bag that was created, I marveled at the change that took place. Each pair of jeans was different in its own way and yet with each one, the transformation was amazing as the old denim was recreated and made into something new. The 'new life' that these jeans now had, reminded me of the very children for whom I was making them. Children, who maybe had been cast aside, unwanted or 'used' by worldly standards but were now rescued, restored and renewed. In Psalm 139 it reads that we are *"fearfully and wonderfully made."* Unfortunately, in life, too many children are not valued and loved in the way that God intended when He fashioned them together in their mother's womb. Thankfully though, when ZOE helps save these precious children from exploitation, abuse and abandonment, their lives are reclaimed and transformed.

Through the Struggle

Between 2001-2003 when I was a teacher at a girls' school in Melbourne, I remember hiring an incubator full of almost-ready-to-hatch eggs. After a day or so of having it in the classroom, the first crack started to appear in one of the eggs and our 'normal' classwork temporarily stopped while sixteen little Grade 2 girls and I stood staring through the glass at the miracle unfolding before our eyes.

It was so exciting to see the little chicks poke their egg tooth through the shell, cracking just a bit at a time. It was hard work for them and the process of getting that shell to crack all the way around and then pushing their bodies out took a huge amount of effort and energy. Sometimes it would get near the end of one of the eggs cracking open and the little chick inside would seem to be running out of energy; desperately pulling on our heat strings as we watched it struggle. But as those of you with experience in chicken hatching know, in most cases, you will do more harm than good in assisting a chick to hatch. Unless you are very experienced and have a complete understanding of what is actually going on inside that shell on a physiological level, your decision to 'help' will most likely have a disastrous effect.

Fast forward to March 2015, when our family stepped out into a new role with the ZOE Transitional Program, every one of the young adults in the program reminded me of those little chicks. Their journey of leaving the children's home and beginning a new stage of life, brought back memories of that overwhelming sense of wanting to 'do more' — the same emotions I had when I pressed my face up against the side of the incubator and watched helplessly as those determined, strong, precious chicks fought and struggled their way out of their shells and into the world. That same, *'I-just-want-to-help-you-break-free-of-that-egg-shell'* feeling of the chicken hatching process, pretty much summed up what I was experiencing. Many times, we were able to offer advice, give counsel, provide help, care, gently redirect and correct ... but really?! There were also a lot of times when, honestly, I just wanted to sit their job interview for them, follow them to work and sort out their concerns or give up my spectator's seat and say, "*I'll take it from here. Let me just crack through that last bit of shell for you and pull you out!"*

In June 2015, during the time we were living at the Transitional Home, our daughter fell over at a local playground and badly broke her arm. When she was in hospital awaiting surgery, her relentless sobbing reduced me to a blubbering mess. Every time they had to find a vein, take blood, x-ray, move her, touch this, prod that, pull that ... my tears started falling. By the time they wheeled her away to the operating theatre, I was completely beside myself. Each time, in those first few days, when I stared into her big blue eyes filled with tears, I would've done anything to take her pain away and have it myself.

"You're so brave" I kept telling her, "I think you're just so brave."

What our family was so privileged to be a part of through those two years living at the Transitional Home, was really the tail-end of so many years of hard work, love and time invested by the parents at ZOE. They had prepared each child for the chance to be free, to see life through new eyes and to step out with restored hope for the future. Parts of the transition process are so beautiful to watch. But other parts are awkward and hard. And whilst many times, we are tempted to say, *"You know what, we'll just do that for you." "We'll fix that problem." "We'll sort that out."* We know that victory and growth and 'life' is often birthed through the struggle. I know that it is through so many of my own challenges, that I have grown stronger in God and more able to stand firm when the next difficulty comes my way.

I love the work ZOE does. Rescuing children, saving them, giving them a chance at a life they were meant to have. We know that their 'time' at ZOE is just so vital and important to their healing and their growth. One night, I sat quietly listening as one of the girls, who lived at the house, bravely shared her feelings of inadequacy and uncertainty about her new job. I was reminded that I could not break the eggshell open for her. I couldn't take away her pain and her insecurities. But I could stand beside her, cheering her on. I could let her know that she is precious, valuable, worthy and loved. And I could keep directing her to the Word, written even before she was born, by the One who created her and who already knew the magnificent plan He had for her life.

A few days after my daughter's arm surgery, as I was brushing her hair for her, she said to me, "Mummy, when I was in the hospital you said something to me that really helped me. I just wanted to say thank you." I immediately paused to look at her. "Thank you for telling me that I was brave," she said. "I didn't feel brave ... but because you said it, it really helped me."

Her words struck me. *"Because you said it."*

What a wonderful reminder of the power of words. As helpless as I feel sometimes when I can't 'fix' the problems and the difficulties I see around me, I can always impact others with words of encouragement. Speaking life and declaring truth to the people whom God places in my circle of influence should be my goal in every season, because those words are how He sees us.

Proverbs 15:23 (ONT) says, *"What a joy it is to find just the right word for the right occasion!"* or in The Message, *"The right word at the right time — beautiful!"*

Beauty in the Mess

Have you ever had a moment in life where you realised that, for whatever reason, you'd believed a lie?

I had an 'ah-ha' moment one day when I suddenly understood that somewhere along the journey, I had wrongly started equating 'beauty' with 'perfection.' I had started to believe that in order to have a beautiful home, it would have to be clean and tidy ... right?! A beautiful face would mean no blemishes ... right?! To be a beautiful family we'd never fight or be grumpy with each other ... right?! I started to believe that to speak Thai beautifully, I'd have to have my tones perfect ... right?! The list went on ...

WRONG! WRONG! WRONG! WRONG!

All of a sudden, I realised that I had created impossible and unrealistic expectations which made me feel so disappointed in myself; questioning why I never seemed to be able to reach my goals. And remember how I mentioned earlier that when we make commitments to ourselves and fail, our dignity takes a hit? Thankfully I recognised the lie which was before me. God revealed that instead of valuing my family, learning new skills or the way He made me, the enemy wanted me to value perfectionism which only led to insecurity about my perceived flaws and weaknesses. Listening to these types of lies would only strengthen the belief that I would never be tidy, pretty or smart enough ... and that I was a failure. But that's not true. That's not at all how God sees me. When I was able to look with fresh eyes and see the beauty in the mess surrounding me, I could finally own the fact that my whole life was one big, beautiful mess! But through that mess, God was at work. My thoughts need to be in line with how He sees me — refusing to agree with anything that's not in the Word of God.

Which then led me to ask, what if I gave myself permission to embrace my mess and see it as an opportunity for loving, learning and growing? What if my family had complete freedom to accept their mess as well? For them to really know that no matter what mistakes they made, what risks they took or what chaos they found themselves in, it would be okay.

They were okay. God still loves them. They are enough.

Could I begin to see 'mess' and the 'imperfection' in a

new way? One day I looked down at my t-shirt and noticed its imperfectly ironed sleeves. To others it might have appeared sloppy on my part, but once you know the story behind those sleeves, you think differently. It's an example of a daughter who knew her mum had been unwell for the past week and saw the mountain of clothes in the room that had not yet been folded, ironed or put away. It's the beautiful account of a ten-year-old girl who, sensing someone else's feelings of being overwhelmed, chose to display self-sacrifice, helpfulness and love.

On the way to school one day, a preteen in our car was particularly anxious. The comments towards the rest of us were unfair and hurtful. They were spoken out of fear and anger and yet through the loud words of insecurity came an unexpected silence by my other two children that I can only identify as the fruit of 'self-control.' As we pulled into the school carpark ... the anxious one muttered words of apology and repentance ... to which we all responded with forgiveness. Without my instruction, these children had demonstrated love and grace. The ranting and the angry words had been unpleasant but yet what came out of it was so beautiful to see.

Another time, Dave and I sat around our table with the kids and decided to try a new tact. Instead of lecturing about not fighting, we acknowledged our disagreements and differences and we agreed on how to fight fairly. How beautiful it is to see that, even in the mess of misunderstanding, we can choose not to put each other down, blame, threaten ... or bring up past mistakes. How beautiful to work together instead of trying to tear down.

In 2016 I began studying the Thai language yet *again!* But this time I started to finally grasp the concept of 'beautiful attempts' as opposed to 'mistakes' ... and 'boldness' as a substitute for 'fear' ... and 'steps closer to my goal' instead of 'setbacks.' What if I could see all my messes and struggles as beautiful moments in disguise? So, when I cringe at my dirty floors, let me be reminded of the laughter, love, responsibility and fun it is to have a pet dog. If I start to shy away from speaking Thai, let me see the beauty in trying, the humour in the mistakes and the resilience that I am developing in not giving up. When my family starts to argue, may I choose to see the powerful beauty in grace, forgiveness, unconditional love and the gift of second chances. As I stare at my reflection in the mornings, may the tired eyes, the smile lines and the sunspots remind me of the beauty in aging, time spent laughing and hours enjoying the outdoors. May the crinkled shirt, the bin not emptied and the pile of socks still not paired, remind me of the rewards of teaching my children responsibility and becoming independent. And may it increase my patience and encouragement towards them.

So now I see ...

... beauty is not perfection!

Beauty is the everyday mess of imperfect people learning, growing and accepting each other. It's dust, wrinkles, dirty dishes, unmade beds and smelly dog bones. But more importantly it's laughter, gentleness, kindness, persistence ... and so much more!

My hope moving forward is that by owning my own mess, I impart to others the courage and freedom to acknowledge theirs too!

New Growth

One school break in spring, we designated a family day to do 'work' in the garden. We had an area that needed to be totally stripped of all the plantings that had been left to grow wildly-out-of-control there, and due to the fact that we were going to try to replant some of them elsewhere in the garden, we needed to uproot these plants carefully.

It was 'all hands-on-deck' as we dug, pulled, sorted and bagged up the branches and stems that we weren't keeping and set aside the ones we were. Slowly the area that was once overgrown looked stark and bare in contrast to just a few hours earlier. An empty space remained. Everything that had once crowded and choked the soil was now gone.

There was another area of the yard that previously had nothing growing there. It's an odd space since not much rain or sun reaches the area. We had decided to move some of our smaller plants that we'd had hanging indoors to this spot and give it a bit more life. With careful hands we dug evenly spaced holes and prepared the ground for the new life it was about to receive.

The words that kept coming to mind throughout the day were, *'out-with-the-old-and-in-with-the new.'*

Afterwards, as I painfully (my muscles were so sore) reflected on that day of gardening, I realised that it had not just been physically exhausting, due to the effort required to remove the plants in such hot weather, but it was the time it took and the chaos of it all that struck me ...

... and strangely it echoed how my life felt at that time.

To make room for new habits, new routines and new thinking, the old must be removed. Sometimes the painfulness of the pulling, the clearing and the sorting out is like a complete make-over; a stripping back of what has always been there, growing wildly-out-of-control. The result after the uprooting and the clearing-out is a stark, blank canvas ... an open space ... an empty basket. It's a new chance.

Although it's hard and exhausting work, this 'stripping away' creates a chance to start again, to begin afresh. It creates new opportunities to replant, more deliberately this time. To consider what is best for this space, to make a decision with the benefit of hindsight and determine what should go in and what should not.

In this process, there is a critical step in the middle which needs to be made. It is not even a step — it is actually a 'pause.' It is this pause, before the replanting begins, that allows time for the preparation of the soil ... for it is the condition of the soil that will ultimately affect the growth.

So quickly our lives can get completely overcrowded and out of control. How difficult it can be, in the busyness of life, to stop long enough to make a change. It's in the 'stopping' — in 'the pause' — that the 'starting to live more purposefully' can begin. The springtime is a perfect time to weed out, regroup and be purposeful about what you will plant and want to put into your life.

Personal Development

At the beginning of one school year, a little six-year-old in our family sat weeping in the car on the way to school. "*I don't want to do my spelling test today. What if I get my words wrong?*"

Fast forward two months, and there I sat, cross-legged on a mat at ZOE, facing a co-worker who was encouraging me to answer the question she'd just asked me in Thai. "Just have a go," she gently prompted but the only words that came out of my mouth were English: "*I can't. What if I get it wrong?*"

There was a certain amount of hopelessness that I felt in the pit of my stomach that day. Not just for me, but also for the mother-in-me who was still struggling with how to get it together enough to help her children let go of their "perfect-or-nothing" mantras. That day as we drove home, I had to make a decision. Going forward ... *change* must come. Spring is a season for pruning, and pruning was what was needed!

Growth always requires pruning. Not to cause us intentional pain but to improve the quality of what we will produce. And so, I asked myself, was I prepared to fail in order to succeed? In order to move forward, was I prepared to let go? Was I ready to break off the chains that held me back so many times? Would I make a change, if not for myself, but for my children whose little eyes watch my every move? On the inside I wept. I was so sorry for all the time I'd wasted holding back due to my own crippling insecurities.

I was sorry about the neighbours whom I never *really* got to know because ... what if I said something wrong? I was sorry about the people cooking food on the side of the street that I feared would laugh at me for saying the wrong classifier when I ordered. I was sorry about the hairdresser who wanted to engage in conversation but instead, I hoped they'd just think I was a tourist ... the list went on.

In the end, there was no point feeling sorry for myself any longer. I needed to take action. I'm not going to lie, but since that day it's been hard not to fall back into old mindsets. But I have been chipping away at my Thai language studies, and I am *very* slowly ... and I mean *VERY* ... slowly, learning and building confidence.

Mentally, every time I begin a block of study, I feel exhausted. Most times I have words swimming around in my head that I don't even know what they mean, only that at some point that day I had learnt to say them. I have been known to ask my teacher, "What did I just say to you?"

What has been the biggest shift though, is that I am beginning to laugh at myself more and loosen up just a bit. Sometimes in Thai classes I have laughed so hard that my cheeks hurt. But actually, it's been okay — even when I've gotten it wrong. It's small baby steps forward, and I know in every area of my life there will be times when I may fall down, but I am determined to get up and try again. I have to keep reminding myself that growth requires trusting in 'the ONE' doing the pruning. He is always close by, ready to show me what new growth looks like after He's clipped and trimmed off the dead wood.

Deep Clean

Is there anyone reading this who thinks that parenting is easy? I think all loving care-givers would agree that intentional parenting is hard work! In March 2020 when I was asked to share with the ZOE parents about what ideas I had about shepherding children's hearts. At that time, our family had an 11, 13 and 14-year-old — plus a 16-year-old exchange student living with us.

For me, the most obvious place to start was in Proverbs 4:23 where it says, the heart is the wellspring of life. One beautiful thing about the Thai language is the emphasis on the heart. The word for heart in Thai is Lil (jai). And Thai has so many words that include the word 'heart.' Here are a few examples: In English we'd say, "*change your mind*" but in Thai it's "*change your heart.*" In English, we'd say "*closed-minded*" but Thai would say you have a "*closed heart.*" In English we say, "*calm down*" but Thai says, "*cool your heart.*" English says, "*to understand*" but in Thai you would say "*enter heart.*" "*Hurt feelings*" translates to "*hurt heart*"; and "*trust*" is "*hold heart*" ... plus there are so many more examples. It's *really* interesting!

I believe that God cares about our hearts and our children's hearts. 1 Samuel 16:7 "For the Lord sees not as man sees: man looks on the outward appearance, but the Lord looks on the heart." Since God cares about our heart, we should care about it too. It is our control center — it's why we are told to guard our hearts.

For me, I think the first step to shepherding the hearts of our children is to focus on our own hearts. It is hard to lead our children's hearts in the ways of God if our hearts are not healthy. We can sit and read our Bible every day, pray every day, daily repent, daily surrender, daily forgive and daily give thanks — but I believe we also need to spend some time deep cleaning!

My first part-time job when I was 15 years old was at the restaurant Sizzler. My area was the salad bar and a big part of my job was to keep the salad bar looking clean and replenished. Every time I worked, I would remember my manager's words, "*Clean as you go.*" But once a month or so, we were all expected to come in to have a deep cleaning night. We would get stuck into cleaning the grout, the tiles, pull out the ice cream machine and wash all the little parts.

So, one thing we can do regularly as parents is to assess the condition of our own heart. What motivates us? Check our heart attitudes. If something is annoying us, it might be an indication of something deeper that we haven't yet seen but that we need to repent of, or forgive, etc. I use questions of self-reflection like: How do I respond during hard times? Am I quick to forgive? Am I putting God first? Am I being ungrateful? Do I criticise or judge others? These are really tough questions. From time to time, I like to use the 'Heart Cleaning' checklist that Pastor Rick Warren developed. This checklist has lots of these questions and Bible verses that help me see what areas I need to work on in my own heart.

Secondly, just like we need to do a spiritual check on our own heart — a 'deep clean' — we can also lead our children in regular heart 'check-ups.' This can be as formal or informal as you like. Maybe around the dinner table at night, during family devotions, while out driving, on the weekend. Study God's word together. Share what God is speaking to you about. Make the time. It's always hard, so you will have to be intentional and most likely sacrifice something else to ensure it happens. We all know that being intentional means that sometimes you have to say 'no' to some things in order to say 'yes' to other things.

With your children, ask the hard questions, the heart-cleansing questions. During family times of discussion, use motivational videos, stories, etc. Reflect on the day with your kids. Did they have any heart struggles? Did they notice any times during the day when they felt God speaking to their heart?

Use God's word to encourage them, not as judgment. Show God's grace, His unconditional love. He is the God of second chances and third chances. Encourage the whole family not to hold grudges. Forgive. Make sure your children hear you say, "*Nothing you can do will make me love you less*" and believe it to be true because this is how God sees and loves them. Many times, children with low self-esteem find it hard to take correction, and so start hating themselves. Try to separate your love and forgiveness with the issue/problem. The problem is the problem — your child is not the problem. We also have our children take turns leading devotions. Some nights they hear from us, other nights they take turns leading and what they share often ministers to their own heart or helps to reveal to us what's in their heart.

Thirdly, recognise and know the difference between the condition of the heart and the behavior you see. This is probably the hardest one for me! A child's behavior can become the focus so easily because it's much more obvious to see, and it gets our attention. Bad behavior can irritate and frustrate us as parents. It's like that well-known image of the iceberg. Imagine what we see on the top of the water is bad behaviour: yelling, hitting, stealing, being bossy, unkind words, etc. But under the surface are the reasons 'why' we can see those behaviors. It's the issues of the heart: jealousy, fear, guilt, shame, feeling inadequate, insecurity, abandonment. There might be fear of being rejected, a belief that they are unworthy of love, grief, anxiety, an offence, worry, disappointment, insecurity, loneliness, shame or guilt. These are just some of the many things that may be lurking under the surface.

Oftentimes as parents we work hard to change the top section of the iceberg! We focus on behaviour modification. We discipline the behaviour but never seek to find the reason beneath the surface. A child's behavior can become the focus because it's much easier to see ... but it is the heart issues that really need the most attention. I think if I was being really honest, I would've said that when my children were little, I thought I was shepherding their hearts ... but actually when I look back, I can think of many instances when I just wanted them to behave in the right way and not be an embarrassment to me.

I would use threats like, "If you don't stop doing that then you'll miss out on... " But usually, I was so frustrated by then, I would say something big and not follow through. Over the years, I have had to train myself not to do that. It sometimes manages the behaviour short-term but does not deal with the heart. I think it's especially important living in a country where we stand out so much. We look different, sound different and there is no being inconspicuous or 'going under the radar' so to speak. There were times I knew I wanted my children to be quiet, polite and do the right thing in public, just so that I felt like a good parent. We must keep remembering that we are going for something bigger — the long-term goal. We must let go of the fear of embarrassment. We are raising mini adults, someone else's future parents! So often as parents it's tempting to think we've solved the problem when we correct the undesirable behavior, but the heart behind the sin hasn't been addressed. It is possible to master some Christian 'performance skills' without experiencing internal change. This is just acting and pretending and soon enough it will be obvious that it was not real change.

I don't want to be a Christian parent who raises 'outwardly compliant children' but who are still rebellious against God in their hearts. I long for authentic change that works from the inside out. This requires digging down and doing the underground work! The hard work. The goals are repentance, reliance on God and lasting transformation, not just compliance ... a changed heart, not just religiously 'following the rules.'

We're never going to know everything that is below the surface, only God knows that; but we must try to connect with our child's heart by getting to know them more, trying to understand what is happening with regard to the things no one else can see. Also, it's important to recognise that understanding the heart behaviour doesn't mean that you approve of their outward behaviour. We still need to address when children do the wrong thing, but doing so from a place of understanding what else is happening ... getting the big picture!

My fourth suggestion for parenting the hearts of children is to address heart issues when the heart is soft. Have you ever tried to reason with kids (or adults!) when they're hot-tempered? They're irrational! They can't think clearly! They seem like they can't 'hear' you ... they are unable to listen! Well, that's when you know it's time to take a break. Make sure people are safe, but don't try to talk about the issue or deal with the problem at that moment. Make a time later when everyone has cooled down. (But be sure you don't forget!!) This is very important. I'm sure you know already but studies show that children can't receive what parents are saying when they are angry, frightened, or even too excited. In fact, none of us make good decisions when our emotions are too big.

When their heart is cool, you can ask heart-probing questions. Jesus asked lots of questions. He used questions to teach truths. I've heard it said, "Jesus never asked a question because He needed to know the answer." He used questions to help us reach a new level of understanding. By asking probing questions, we let children see and take ownership of their heart. If we just tell them "Don't do this..." they are not learning to discern their hearts.

One day my little one was in church wearing a pair of uncomfortable skinny-leg jeans. He kept squirming and bumping me wanting to get my attention so that I'd know all about his discomfort. I was trying to focus on the sermon and at the same time think about my response. Should I take him out? Does he need to go to the bathroom and re-adjust? Eventually I calmly and quietly leaned over, "I can see that you're uncomfortable. What do you want me to do?" But he realised in that moment that there was nothing to do but endure. Once he answered the question for himself, he took ownership of the problem! Like when my children were little (or last week even) when they asked me for something without using proper manners, I can give them the opportunity to fix the mistake. If I say, "try again" it means that they have to come up with a solution as opposed to me giving the answer, "You didn't say please."

Lastly, find ways to connect with each child individually. Maybe they like quality time with you playing card games or eating snacks while hearing you read. Some children love physical touch: snuggling, shoulder massages and wrestling, or they appreciate acts of service when you help them out with something. Win their heart. I've mentioned how, with one of my children, when I need to reach his heart, I go with food. With another I use physical touch to soften their heart. Sometimes I'll even use technology with my teens. Send an email, text message, scripture, encouragement. Remaining connected with our children and finding delight in understanding them is key.

And lastly, *lastly!* ... practise speaking life over them and teaching them to speak life too. If a child lies, remind them "You are not a liar! You are a child of God who can walk in truth."

Love them and try to see them the way God does.

Above all else: pray, pray, pray ... and intercede on behalf of your kids and have faith. This is necessary when it comes to raising children. We can provide a good influence and do all we can to help them and guide them towards God, but at the end of the day we must entrust them to God.

Stop and Smell the Roses

Whenever I drive through a particular area of the city, I feel reminiscent about when we lived there. There were some significant lessons that we learnt in that little two-bedroom city house. It represented a season of change where we were being challenged to keep pushing the boundaries of our comfort level. I was remembering back to one of the times that some of the ZOE kids had come over to our house. This particular time, the youth had an outing but some of the teenagers were unable to go, so they had arranged to come to our house for pizza and to play Wii Sport. We'd sat around on the tile floor laughing and eating. Once dinner was complete, I was impressed by their initiative to pack up and clean up the area where we'd been sitting. After we'd all pitched in, Dave set up the Wii and for the next couple of hours we sat around watching and laughing as we all took turns skiing, tightrope walking, hula hooping etc.

As the night wore on, our usually hyperactive young son slowly began to become weary. After his turn, he nestled into the lap of one of the teenage boys and sat there so at ease and comfortable and unusually calm. I remember looking over and smiling. It was one of the boys whom I had taught in my English class many months earlier. He had begun in my class not long after arriving at ZOE. I literally had needed to coax him out from under the table and teach him to sit at a desk.

What struck me as I remembered back fondly on this time was the way in which my young son, not knowing the details of this teenage boy's past, was able to see him for who he was. I think so often as adults, we look through lenses of pity, horror, sadness or the world's standards of success and attractiveness. It's hard to see the beauty that God sees in each person, both to recognise it in our own life and to search for it in other's lives.

In the season of spring, we start to notice that there *is* beauty all around us. A seemingly scrawny rose bush in our driveway will one day catch my eye as it shows off the splendor of its lovely new white petals. The smell of freshly cut grass tingles my nostrils after the absence of being cut in the winter and the appearance of baby animals in fields, gathering close to their mother's side, grabs my attention as I drive around. Part of this season and the calmness it brings is in the stopping and the noticing. I don't have a lot of flowers in my garden ... but when I see a rose in bloom, I stop.

I stop ... and I smell the roses.

And it should remind me that there are 'roses' everywhere ... all throughout my day but I need to slow down enough to notice them. They may look like children or friends, or perhaps even strangers, but they are beautiful to God; and in turn when I am present enough to look for them, I come to see they are beautiful to me too. I get a glimpse into who they are, noticing and deeply appreciating them. Spring is not a time to let things pass us by. It's so important to stop and smell the roses!

Letting Go

As I have stated before, we have moved house so many times since living in Thailand. This one occasion though, back in 2014, when we were right in the middle of the messy stage of sorting and packing; our young children had just seen the hugely successful animated movie, *Frozen.* For you other parents, I'm sure you can also remember the movie and, of course, its catchy tunes. But there was one song in particular that was sung quite frequently around our house all those years ago. Can you guess what it was? Yep! *"Let it go ... Let it go."*

This song, which interestingly was translated into 41 different languages for the film's foreign release, became sort of like a 'mantra' for us during those weeks of deciding what to take, what to toss and what to give away. With less than a week until moving day, there were cupboards being sorted and drawers being cleaned out in just about every room. Everything was up for discussion as to whether it would stay or whether it would go. And so, as I sat cross-legged on my children's bedroom floor holding up one precious piece of artwork, or one keepsake after another — along with many not-so-precious-items that had been hoarded since the last time we had moved house — the kids and I would ask ...

"Keep it or let it go?"

And thankfully, over the years we have gotten better at replying, *"Let it go!"* which was often followed by at least one, if not all of us, bursting into song.

Amusing as it was, I found it rather surprising that it took a Disney cartoon to lead me to more serious thoughts about 'letting go' of things. It not only helped me sort through my material possessions, but it also challenged me about what was in my heart and my life that also needed a big cleanout.

"Oh, I don't have *that much*" I told myself defensively, "Just that old grudge, that one hidden hurt, those boxes of disappointments, that drawer full of comparisons and that closet full of unrealistic expectations." Oh, but I'd forgotten. There were also all those worries and that guilt that was stacked up high on the shelf; not to mention the shed full of discouragement and inhibitions that I'd just shut the door on, hoping they'd go away by themselves. As I started to examine all the 'junk' I'd collected emotionally, it started to feel like the clearing out of the clutter *in my heart* was going to be harder than trying to hit the high notes whilst attempting to sing the Oscar-winning ballad "Let it Go."

It was also during this period of time that I learnt so much from my young children. They had all been given some money from a very generous supporter in America. Unsure as to what they wanted to use it for, the money was left sitting there in the envelope in which it came. And then our church began a project called 'Kids Aren't Trash,' where some children, who had been living and working on a toxic waste dump, were rescued and given a home. Our church started asking for donations, which immediately sparked my children's interest. Using all their money, they bought Hot Wheels cars, toothbrushes and underwear; and then they went through their own precious belongings to find teddy bears, clothes and other bits and pieces that they wanted to give.

Why would they do this? Spend all their money and give their toys to kids they'd never met? Well, I believe it's because they were starting to understand that even when they give it all or let it go, they know deep down in their hearts that they're going to be okay. And that holding loosely to their *'stuff'* and caring about people is far more rewarding than the reverse. And that letting go often means getting back far more than we can imagine.

Then ... after all *that* giving ... our precious daughter had decided to have 35cm of her beautiful long blonde hair cut off to send to Australia to be made into a wig for someone who was battling cancer. If you knew our little girl you'd know that she LOVED her long hair. If I ever even *suggested* or threatened, as I battled through the knots on a daily basis before school, that she should *maybe* just consider having it trimmed, she would burst into uncontrollable tears. So, when she came to me, weeks after we'd been praying for a little nine-year-old girl in our church network who was going through chemotherapy and explained what she wanted to do. I was shocked! *Really* shocked!! Why would she want to do that? My children were learning. They could already see that letting something go and giving something up doesn't mean losing out. She was so happy that her hair would be used to help someone else.

I have much to learn from these little people in my life. These children who make loom bands for kids in Africa or meet strangers and freely give their boxed milk away at the park. Sometimes as adults it's so difficult to let go of the 'stuff' that we hold so tightly. We grip it so firmly, unsure as to whether we trust God enough to stop leaning on our own understanding in the situation. I'm so glad that I don't *have* to keep all my emotional junk. That there is someone so much greater than all I have who *wants* to take it off my hands, someone who is more than enough for me.

When God reaches down to help me, am I going to be awkwardly holding onto my junk, fumbling to keep it all close by, or will I have my hands free to accept His help? I believe He wants to say lovingly to us today, "It's time to put all that stuff down. Let it go!" His hand is outstretched waiting for us to grab hold of it and to receive His help, which we all need so desperately. He never meant for us to do life alone or try to manage our problems in our own way, and our own strength.

So, I sit here again reminded to ask, what else do I need to just say, *"Let it go..."* to?

Scraps

Our family started down a different dietary path in 2015 when one of our children had some health and wellness concerns. We were curious to see whether eliminating certain foods would make any difference. What happened actually amazed us ... but that's a whole different story. Since that time, I have been on a steep learning curve to adapt recipes, substitute ingredients and create new ways of doing things with our family's meals. In the beginning, I felt completely overwhelmed, but now I can cook from a place of increased confidence, experiment with new ingredients, and actually enjoy the experience.

There's something very satisfying about cooking from scratch and knowing exactly what we're eating. We have this restaurant that we really like going to for special occasions. It's not fancy but their food is really good quality. I had mentioned to our children one day how I like it because everything there is 'made from scratch', which is how *we* like to cook. Upon repeating part of this conversation a week or so later one of our kids very earnestly said, "It's because everything there is 'made from *scraps*'!"

We all had a good laugh.

Do you ever have those weeks or months where life just feels busy, busy, busy? It might even be 'good' busy with friends visiting, basketball tournaments, class parties, work functions, concerts and projects to finish. Sometimes I wonder though, despite *wanting* my life to reflect the quality of a wonderful healthy meal made from scratch, how upon closer examination, it can sometimes resemble a bit of a mess — more like a meal made from scraps!

Scraps of time, half-finished conversations, unfinished prayers, incomplete jobs, emails sitting in the draft folder ...

anyone else?

And whilst I don't want God and my family to just 'get my leftovers' at the end of the day, the small fragments of time that might be left, the scraps after everything else has been used up are sometimes all I feel like I have to offer. I was challenged recently when I read the following article by Scott DeVries:

'God is our greatest authority. We wouldn't give our earthly authorities our scraps. Yet so often we offer God the leftover portions of our time, money, energy, thought, and emotion. He gets the scraps and rejects — just as the Israelites were offering the worst of their animals in sacrifice.

It must have been a burden to care for a blind or lame animal. The temptation to sacrifice such an animal would be very real. Wouldn't a blind or lame animal suit God — purposes just as well as any other animal?

We face a similar temptation. We pray with the five extra minutes we might have and aren't sure what else we can do with that time. We help with a service project on a Saturday that is "free" on our calendar: We're happy to tithe as long as we have some disposable income. We read that deep religious book, if we're in between novels.

We have to admit, though, that extras aren't really sacrifices. When we willingly sacrifice time, money, or energy that has value to us, it settles the greater value of God into our hearts and minds. God sacrificed his only Son for us. Certainly he is far more worthy of our best than any earthly authority.'

[https://todaydevotional.com/devotions/giving-god-our-scraps]

Several years ago, during a visit to ZOE, an international speaker taught some sessions and challenged the Thai staff and foreign volunteers to keep asking smart questions. He referred to a study which showed the average 4-year-old British girl asks her mother about 390 questions a day; yet by the time we are adults though the number of questions most of us ask per day has dwindled incredibly.

Knowing that God, and my family, are worth more than *my* scraps, I challenge myself with these questions:

How do I show God that He is 'Number 1' in my life? What's getting in my way of focusing on God?

How am I showing my family that I love them?

Are they receiving my sacrifices of 'love' or do I need to find alternative ways to reach their hearts?

A Young Boy

One dinnertime in 2018, we sat around eating and discussing many different things going on in life. Then we started talking about how we needed someone to come and work for ZOE in Australia. We discussed many aspects of the job, and Dave mentioned that it would cost a lot of money to pay the person, until our daughter reminded us — matter-of-factly — that God would provide.

Our youngest son left the table at that point and we thought he'd gone to the bathroom, but when he returned, he had something stuffed under his t-shirt. With tear-filled eyes, he started pulling cash out from under his top. "This is all my money that I was saving to spend in Australia but I want to give it to ZOE for the person that we need." We assured him that he didn't need to but he insisted that he *wanted* to. On reflection, it reminded me of the story in the Bible when Jesus Feeds the Five Thousand.

The disciples came to Jesus saying, "There is no food around here and it's already getting late. Maybe we should send the people away so they can go to the surrounding towns and get themselves something to eat." (Matthew 14:15) But Jesus replied, "They do not need to go away. You give them something to eat." Instead of remembering the water that had been turned into wine, and Jesus' ability to provide, the disciples wonder "how?' But this little boy, with a small food offering, makes his way over to one of the disciples and in John 6:8 Andrew speaks up, "Here is a boy with five small loaves of bread and two small fish, but how far will they go among so many people?" Jesus took the loaves of bread and thanked God for them. Then the disciples passed around the bread and everyone had enough. Next, He did the same with the fish. Those five small loaves of bread and two small fish fed five thousand people!

How often when faced with situations do we get carried away asking "But how?" We question, "Don't you realise how expensive that will be God?" Like He needs us to set the budget or tell Him what to do!

We knew that just like the boy with his lunch offering, our son's 'seed' had been planted. His offering was also multiplied and God showed us down the track that He had more than enough. David helped our son donate his money through the ZOE website and we knew that God would not only enlarge his offering, but He would also bring the right person for the job in His time. A year-and-a-half later, that person sat at our dinner table with us and we were able to share the wonderful story of a little boy's offering with them and God's faithfulness to bless and multiply it.

Just like the boy with his fish lunch, our small boy was generous to share what he had, with faith, knowing that God would do the rest. What was challenging for the rest of us was being reminded to be obedient to what God was telling *us* to do. Since our son's act of generosity, others were also prompted to bless those around them with what was in their hands. God is looking for our willingness to release what we have into His. He will perform the miracle of multiplication and make our little gift — *enough*. What if that small thing, clutched so closely, could actually be used for something amazing? We know God will demonstrate again and again that He *has* and He *is* more than enough!

Off the Beaten Track

We went on a hike one weekend with friends. It's always amusing to see all the different personalities emerge and watch all of the individual ways of handling this kind of adventure, or challenge, as it was for some. Ralph Waldo Emerson said, "Do not go where the path may lead, go instead where there is no path and leave a trail." I like that.

Some of us love the wild and unpredictable, the idea of getting lost, the places where there is no path and the challenge of the unmarked journey. Others of us like to know the plan, how long the journey will take, where we can stop and what snacks there are to eat. You get the picture! What fascinates me though is that how we relate to 'life' in general does not always correspond to how we approach a hike. Take me, for example. In general, I do like to know the plan. I try to be organised and prepared. I like to be punctual and complete tasks within a set time frame. But on a hike, the thought of getting lost excites me, the fact that we don't know which way we're going or what time we'll finish brings out the carefree side of me, and that it's refreshing to be reminded that there are times when it's okay to not rush ... to not know ... or not to have a plan. And sometimes it takes getting off the beaten track to remember that.

"Of all the paths you take in life, make sure a few of them are dirt." - John Muir

I must say, I really enjoyed that hike. Despite the fact I was so hot and sweaty by the end, sometimes my muscles ached and the long grass against my skin made me itchy. But that road-less-travelled, was a moment in time to be surrounded by nature and see interesting bugs and creatures in their natural environment (instead of seeing them in my kitchen for a change!) And to be lost ... lost in the physical sense of not really knowing which direction we were going ... but also lost in thought. And sometimes that's exactly when everything starts to make more sense and become clearer. It's like we get a new way of seeing everything.

How come I don't make the time to wander, explore and to connect in this different way more often? I love these opportunities to disconnect and clear my mind of the normal, everyday stresses. And I know that it's something our family needs to do more often too.

Remembering the Source

There's a quote that says, 'A mother is only as happy as her least happy child' and while I fully understand *that;* I want to also expand it and say that when my husband went through a very dark and wintery season beginning in 2017, our family seemed like it could only be as happy as our least happy family member. Our leader, our encourager, our funny-man, our capable head, our front-runner ... was suddenly out of position — lost and down. It was the knockout punch that none of us saw coming. 1, 2, 3, 4, 5 ...

Throughout that season, but in particular for the first four to six months (which were the hardest), I had to learn to trust God in a new way. That 'cord of three strands' that I had envisioned on our wedding day, literally felt like it was a tattered piece of frayed rope that might just break at any second ... 6, 7, 8 ...!

Despite the 'shabbiness' of the rope, and our circumstances, I learnt to look to the *only* One who could carry me through that time and bring change where it was needed. Each day, alone in my car, through tear-filled eyes, I would entrust my husband to God, not knowing what outcomes would emerge, or what situation I would find when I returned home — but confident that He who loved us so much, and that He had us all in His hands.

As 2017 drew to a close, the darkness over Dave, and the shadows that had been cast over our family, gradually started to lift. It was the 'spring' I described in the opening paragraph. Slowly the puddles began to dry up and the colour that had all but disappeared began to be unveiled once again. A giggle, a faint smile, a connection, a purpose and ever so slowly 'hope' began to creep its way back into our home again. And although, like a boxer, he felt beat-up and bruised emotionally, physically and spiritually, Dave had beaten the count down and got back into the fight once again.

You would think that with the spring and the glimpses of new life and fresh starts, that my heart would have leapt with joy and gratitude ... and to a degree it did. But what caught me off-guard with this new season of optimism and anticipation was a sneaky case of discontent that had crept in when I was least expecting it.

There are no excuses. But I do think that in the dark times and the pressing moments, it was almost an all-consuming 'survivor' type of mentality that had driven me to keep going and never give up. "Be strong for the kids," "Keep it all together." But when the foot eases off the accelerator and we don't have to push so hard, when we can just cruise a little and not focus so much on the road, that's when we can dangerously start to fall into a trap of becoming too fixated on things around us that we hadn't even noticed or let bother us before.

There's a story in Luke 17:11 where Jesus heals ten men with leprosy. They had begged for Jesus to have mercy on them. Out of the ten, who were all healed that day, do you know how many came back to show Jesus a bit of gratitude? Only 1 ... *one* ... ONE! Out of ten, only one came back to say thank you. And I ask myself, how often do I beg and cry out "Jesus, Master, have pity on *me*. Help meeeeee!" But then, when I get my miracle, when I see healing and provision and His goodness, where am I? Why do I so quickly forget the source? How can I not come running back into His arms, saying:

Praise the Lord, my soul;
all my inmost being, praise His holy name.
Praise the Lord, my soul,
and forget not all His benefits —
who forgives all your sins and heals all your diseases,
who redeems your life from the pit
and crowns you with love and compassion,
who satisfies your desires with good things
so that your youth is renewed like the eagle's.

Psalm 103: 1-5 (NIV)

Why do I have to be so much like the Israelites who saw the supernatural answers to their prayers and then turned to grumble and complain? When I realised what had happened, when I suddenly saw how ugly my short-lived utterances of 'praise and thanks' for the healing and restoration I had witnessed in Dave's life were; compared to how quickly I moved into, *"Our house is too small!" "Why are there rats?" "This bench is too low!" "Our kitchen is too hot!"* ... I really had to confess and repent for having such a spirit of ungratefulness.

From that moment, I worked on being thankful for even the things around me that were frustrations, choosing to see the good, focusing on the positive and making the most of the situation. What happened within a matter of weeks was so unexpected, that I feel even worse for having had such a bad attitude; but as my heart changed and I started to see things differently, God unlocked provision beyond what I could have ever even hoped for. You see our gratitude, faith and trust in Him keeps the channel of His favour open. He wants us to be thankful in *all* circumstances. Let's be that one who comes running back to give thanks without needing to be reminded and not be one of the others who leaves Jesus asking, "Where are the other nine?"

Fleas

Springtime is a time to practice lessons of reliance on Him and not to trust in our own understanding. Through our thankfulness and by appreciating the blessings of fruitfulness we can believe that the 'pruning' being done is for our benefit and growth.

I don't want to be someone who only thanks God when He does miracles and answers prayers just the way I want, either. It's pretty easy to be thankful when we look around and our lives are going well. But when our situation seems hopeless, and we're struggling through heartbreak and loss, when we don't know where the money for school fees is going to come from or our visa application is denied. It can seem hard to believe that God is really there taking care of things. It can be hard to say, "I know You love me. Thank you for what You are doing even now."

In her book *The Hiding Place,* Corrie Ten Boom tells of a time she discovered that God was working even in the most horrific circumstances. Corrie and her sister Betsie had been imprisoned in a concentration camp by the Nazis for hiding Jews in their home. Corrie writes:

"It grew harder and harder. Even within these four walls there was too much misery, too much seemingly pointless suffering. Every day something else failed to make sense, something else grew too heavy." Yet, in the midst of the suffering, the women prisoners around Corrie and Betsie found comfort in the little Bible studies they held in the barracks. When they were moved to Barracks 28, Corrie was horrified by the fact that their reeking, straw-bed platforms swarmed with fleas. How could they live in such a place? It was Betsie who discovered God's answer: *"'Rejoice always, pray constantly, give thanks in all circumstances; for this is the will of God in Christ Jesus. 'That's it, Corrie! That's His answer. 'Give thanks in all circumstances! 'That's what we can do. We can start right now to thank God for every single thing about this new barrack!"* They thanked God for the fact they were together. They thanked God they had a Bible. They even thanked God for the horrible crowds of prisoners, that more people would be able to hear God's Word. And then, Betsie thanked God for the fleas.

"The fleas!" This was too much. "Betsie, there's no way even God can make me grateful for a flea."

"'Give thanks in all circumstances,' she quoted. "It doesn't say, 'in pleasant circumstances.' Fleas are part of this place where God has put us."

And so they stood between tiers of bunks and gave thanks for fleas. But this time Corrie was sure Betsie was wrong. It turned out though that Betsie was not wrong; the fleas were a nuisance, but a blessing after all. The women were able to have Bible studies in the barracks with a great deal of freedom, never bothered by supervisors coming in and harassing them. They finally discovered that it was the fleas that kept those supervisors out."

Through those fleas, God protected Corrie and Betsie from abuse and harassment. So many desperate women were free to hear the comforting, hope-giving Word of God. Through those fleas, God protected the women in Barracks 28 from much worse things and made sure they had their deepest needs met.

My 'fleas' may look different from yours. We all have those 'things' which are annoyances, frustrations, hardships, or discomforts that make it hard to keep a good attitude. No one's life is free of 'fleas,' but if Corrie and her sister Betsie can be thankful amongst *real* fleas, surely we can come to expect that God will work through our difficulties, using them for our protection and blessing too.

Just Do It

When I first became pregnant in late 2004, I had no idea what this amazing baby that was wiggling and jiggling inside me would be like, or just how much of an incredible person I was about to give birth to. His due date was in early springtime but as that date came (and went) he hadn't arrived yet. The anticipation of that new life to come, mixed with the feeling that winter would never end, (or in my case, 'pregnancy') started to set in. But just like those early spring days which *do* get a little less cold and the changing seasons burst forth with new life, so too did my world as new life was birthed into our home as David and I suddenly transformed into parents.

The day my precious first-born came into this world actually ended up being one of the most stressful days of my life — let's just say the event didn't go quite as I had planned for, or practiced, in antenatal classes. When my son turned thirteen, I reflected back on his birthday that springtime of 2005, and all the things that I wanted him to know and tuck away in his heart as he entered into a new season of his life as a teen.

Firstly, I wanted him to understand that not everything turns out the way we think it will in life. Even though he didn't come into the world in the conventional way that we'd imagined he would, God still had a plan and He was still in control. God was with me and He was also with him even then, as a baby, and He is still with him today. I want my son to come to understand that he can trust and rely on God.

Secondly, because God is with him, *he* can be strong. Our son has already shown his natural 'strength' and resilience in many areas of his life. Although he is still working on physically developing his muscles, he definitely has an inner strength that has seen him through many challenges. But what I wanted my son to know was what it says in 2 Corinthians 12:9, that God's grace is sufficient for him and that when he is aware of his weaknesses and he humbly receives grace, then he will become strong, for God's strength is made perfect in our weakness.

Thirdly, I don't ever want him to stop believing in himself or feel like he is not enough. Because of Jesus, he *is* enough. We are all worthy and valuable. God has given my son many gifts and abilities to use for a purpose. These gifts are an invitation to partner with God, take part in His plan and glorify the Gift-Giver. As a family member, I can already see that he is clever, funny, creative, sweet, gentle, friendly, considerate, perceptive and joyful. Learning to use his gifts for the right reason and for the purpose God has, will be discovered in time.

Finally, if other people tell him what he can't do — I want him to seek God's will and trust in Him alone. With God, nothing is impossible. Together they will be unstoppable.

A lot of the time, my kids wear second-hand clothing because it saves money ... it's eco-friendly and helps people in the community. However, for his birthday, I bought my son a new Nike t-shirt, purely because of the well-known slogan:

'Just Do It.'

What I wanted my son to think about as he wore that slogan, was what the word *'It'* represented. Because ... *'It'* is not what everyone is doing. *'It'* is not just what you feel like doing.

'It' is the plan that God has.

'It' is the right thing, and we can know this in our heart by reading God's word.

I pray that my son (and our whole family) will continue to seek God and keep asking Him to know what the *'it'* is for our lives ... and then *JUST DO IT!*

Check For Yourself

My son loves the predictable. He is someone who wants to be told 'the plan.' He thrives on routine and knowing what to expect. Ever since a young age, he's cringed at the thought of crazy hair, wear-your-pajamas-to-school or dress-as-your-favourite-book-character days. Even at five years of age, when everyone had to dress up as a book character, he wore his uniform to school, took his costume in his school bag and *only* got changed once he saw *for-sure* that everyone else was dressed up.

Even though he's older now, you can imagine how much he loves 'Spirit Week' — *not!* During Spirit Week, students participate in various activities. It's a tradition showing school pride in anticipation of the upcoming Annual Invitational Basketball Tournament with local schools. Students wear different themed clothes each day, compete in contests and each day has a particular focus. My son was relieved one year because on Pajama Day he was out of school at an interschool athletics competition and then on Crazy Hair Day, he had an all-day soccer tournament.

So, the night before 'Dress-as-Your-Favourite-Superhero Day' in February 2017, I didn't even consider that he would *want* to participate. I took my other two children to a second-hand clothes shop to search for Princess Leia and Luke Skywalker type clothing. Then that night, the costumes were put together and laid out ready for the next morning.

Well, come the next morning, Luke Skywalker didn't seem so appealing to my youngest son and he decided (last minute) on just wearing his Captain America t-shirt and a pair of shorts. Seriously?! Trying to remain calm though, and just go-with-the-flow (aka *'get the kids out the door by no later than 7:10 am or else hit super-bad traffic'*). I was totally surprised when my *'I-never-want-to-dress-up'* son pipes up and says, "If you don't want to wear it, then I will."

"Whaaaaaaat?!"

So in shock ... we all encouraged him that *"yes that's a great idea!"* and after he puts it on; we all agree how awesome he looks ... he actually really looks like Luke Skywalker (okay so I don't *really* know because I had never watched Star Wars but anyway, he looks how I'd imagined Luke to look like!)

"But wait!" he announced, starting to pull out his laptop to double check that it *was actually* 'Dress-as-Your-Favourite-Superhero Day.' "Yes, yes" I replied. "No need to check. I have been talking to all the other mothers about it. It's definitely 'Dress-as-Your-Favourite-Superhero Day.' Let's go!" I declare, hurrying him along.

Oh, how I wish the story ended there ... and that I could just say how great everyone looked, and what a fun day the kids all had! However, only five minutes after being dropped off at the front of school, my son made his way back to the front office, tears welling, cheeks burning and every reason why you should NEVER! EVER! Wear a dress-up to school (EVER!) whirling through his mind.

"Marrm!" I heard his shaky voice on the other end say, "Middle-schoolers *don't* wear 'Dress-as-Your-Favourite-Superhero' clothes today. That was just for elementary!"

"What?" Shocked, I reached for my computer to check the schedule on the website. And then just as I found the page, I heard his voice at the same time, "They wear formal clothes today."

Oh no! I instructed him to stay right there at the office.

You can only imagine how upset he was. And I was upset too. Why hadn't I let him check? I was so sure it was all the same. I guess we all got so carried away in how great he looked and how brave he was, suddenly doing something so out of his comfort zone and all. Let's just say that when you're a middle-schooler and half your friends are dressed in formal wear and the other half (who were too nervous to dress up at all) are wearing casual clothes and you're standing there all dressed in white flowing robes with a brown belt holding your toy lightsaber in place ... it's hard to be all like, "What? Yes! This is what I wear to formal gatherings... " Ummm. NOPE! Not happening.

I'm all for bouncing back ... getting back on the horse ... giving it another go ... here's some formal clothes, now get back to school. But I realized, none of those phrases were going to work this time.

"Just stay home buddy!" I said. Poor kid!!

I'm not sure if you've ever had a similar experience. Maybe it wasn't a school theme day but a fancy dress party. And if you haven't, I'm sure you can *imagine* how embarrassing it would've felt.

As I mulled over this event later, I had to laugh. I mean it is pretty funny looking back, right? But then it struck me when I was reading in the Old Testament book of Judges the other day.

> "... *all the people did whatever seemed right in their own eyes.*" Judges 21:25

I started imagining someone who 'dressed' a particular way. Someone who goes through life with everyone around them saying how great they look? How they really look like the 'real deal.' The praise from others carries them through life thinking everything is going as planned. Everything is good. They are doing what is 'right' in their own eyes and maybe even the eyes of their friends, their family and the 'world.'

But then they pass from this earth and reach their Maker ... and when they stand and account for their life, their actions, their choices ... they suddenly realise that they *weren't* dressed the right way at all. They hadn't checked. They had just listened to those around them, never seeking the truth for themselves. And I have to ask myself:

> How many times do I gauge how well I'm doing by the opinions and comments of others?

> How often do I listen and take on the identity that others tell me I am? How regularly do I 'check' what God says as opposed to what my friends, the media or Facebook are saying to me?

> How well do I know what pleases Him as opposed to what seems right to my friends or the world? How dreadful, at the end of it all, to think ...

> If only I'd checked. If only I had taken the time to read the instructions for myself!

Simply put, God invites each of us into relationship with Himself through Jesus. He wants us to willingly love Him and obey His commands. God doesn't ask us to obey just because it is good for Him, but because it is good for *us.* How easy it is to get caught up 'in the moment' ... 'in life' ... 'in what others say is okay' and just forget. If only we would keep checking the source of truth for ourselves.

"Do not be conformed to this world, but be transformed by the renewal of your mind, that by testing you may discern what is the will of God, what is good and acceptable and perfect."

Romans 12:2 [ESV]

The Power of Three

Do you have a favourite number? I don't really, but for some reason though, the number '3' seems to come up a lot. Like ... I am one of three children and I have three children.

And, strangely, I often find myself at the supermarket subconsciously buying grocery items in threes.

Of course, for people with a Christian faith, the number '3' has significance. God is three-in-one — Father, Son and Holy Spirit. Peter denied Jesus three times (Luke 22:54-62). A cord of three strands is not easily broken (Ecclesiastes 4:12) ... and that is just to mention a few examples from over 460 other times the number '3' is mentioned in the Bible.

When I recently heard a song by Hillsong Young & Free from their album (named *Three),* the words of the song impacted me greatly and I was, once again, reminded of how significant this number is in my life.

It's called "Jesus Loves Me" — you can listen to it on YouTube. Maybe you know the older version:

Jesus loves me this I know,
For the Bible tells me so.
Little ones to Him belong
They are weak but He is strong.

For me, it's one of those songs that feels like it's been a part of my life since before I can even remember. And, as a parent, I can recall bedtimes when my children were much smaller — times when I had no words of comfort left of my own and all I could do was to stroke their hair gently and sing those lyrics quietly over them.

What was interesting to find out was that those beautiful old words first appeared as a poem in the context of an 1860 novel, spoken as a comforting poem to a dying child, but the tune was added in 1862. After publication as a song, it became one of the most popular Christian hymns in churches around the world, especially among children.

And now, this updated version of the song is bringing fresh reminders for our family of those comforting and life-changing truths, speaking life and love into our lives during both the best and worst of days.

As a parent, I have days when I feel like most of my conversations involve me saying, "You need to change that...," "More of this ..." "Less of that ..." "Don't do that ..." "Do this ..."

But at the end of the day when my advice, warnings, recommendations, commands and instructions are left ringing in their ears — all I really want my children to know is one thing ... that I love them.

When they're all grown up, more than anything else I want them to reflect back and know that they were loved. More than helping them with homework, more than baking yummy treats, more than the toys and clothes I bought them, more than the lectures, more than the acts of service, words of encouragement and physical affection ... my heart cries out for them to know three words ...

"I love you!"

I think what is so special about this old song is that those three simple words sum everything else up, "Jesus Loves Me."

Maybe for some people, this message is hard to accept. For some, it may seem inconceivable or unbelievable. If that's you, then I invite you test it out this week. Simply ask Jesus to show you His love. It could be life changing. I know it has been for me.

Some of our most substantial growth happens in the midst of spring, and I am beginning to value the significance of this season for its pruning and new growth. I don't want to hold on too tightly to the 'branches' that God wants to trim back or cut off. I want to embrace all that He has for me and prepare for the fruitfulness of summer and respond to what He is calling me to do. I want to be able to recognise the moments that I need to unplug from the cares of this world and reconnect with the One who holds the whole world in His hands. I don't want to miss precious moments with my family because I am distracted or too busy to offer them anything else but my scraps. Through it all, I will trust and be thankful. Through every season I will declare: *"He is Lord over all!"*

We need each season. The loss of autumn sets us up for the uncertainty of winter, which in turn is necessary for the hope, and new growth of spring, which leads to the fruitfulness of summer. Basically, you can't have one without the other. New growth comes from the pruning — and so hope comes from the waiting.

At the start of this journey, I shared Psalm 23:6 (TPT) where it says, "*So why would I fear the future? For your goodness and love pursue me all the days of my life.*" And that's it in a nutshell. He loves you. He pursues you. You *can* feel His presence in every season, as you live with a heart of praise and a decision to worship intentionally regardless of the circumstances, or season, you find yourself in. Start now by inviting His presence and living your life with no fear of winter!

Covid 19

The years 2020-21 will definitely go down as years we will never forget! No one could have predicted the rippling worldwide effect that Covid-19 would have. The virus changed many aspects of our lives. We had to adopt new habits, new priorities and new ways throughout those years, and these undoubtedly influenced how we responded during the unpredictable seasons we faced. Whist in previous years, festivities centred around social gatherings and bustling shopping streets, 2020 provided a chance for us to reflect and reclaim what we truly valued. Many people have shared that during isolation and lockdown, they developed an appetite to *'do'* better and *'be'* better. New hobbies and habits were formed and relationships were explored in different, and inventive ways. But I think it also gave people the chance to reflect and consider what had been lost in the past, how we'd missed the mark in regard to what was *really* important, and how our actions influence others. I saw this especially during Christmas 2020.

The imposed restrictions and the changing world gave Christians an opportunity to open our hearts and hear what God wanted to do new and fresh in our lives. And what reclaiming Christmas actually looked like.

Maybe, just like Mary and Joseph, it was remembering to trust in God especially when faced with unforeseen challenges.

Maybe, like the shepherds, whose lives were transformed when they understood what Jesus' birth meant — we saw that our lives really could impact the people around us.

Maybe it was being generous by sharing God's love with

neighbours and our community. Maybe it was taking time to pause and reflect on the miracle that is 'God-among-us'.

Maybe it was sharing the gift of ourselves with the lonely and those in our circle of family and friends who'd gain more from the gift of our 'presence' rather than an off-the-shelf present.

Maybe it was about getting back to basics and celebrating the LIFE of Christ in a simple yet meaningful way.

As you reflect back on 2020, and the other times of lockdown since, maybe you didn't experience much joy. You felt tired. You felt depressed. You were isolated. You experienced loss. You had personal tragedy and difficulties that filled you with grief, sorrow and frustration.

Do you know God was with you? He saw. You are so valuable to Him. You are worthy of Him sending His one and only Son. If you haven't received His free gift yet, it's not too late.* He can give you the forgiveness, strength, help, and victory you need. 2020 was a great reminder to do things differently and reclaim what was lost. God's dream is for this world to experience His abundant (zoe) LIFE.

*turn to the end of this book for how to do this

Proverbs 31

I've always liked my name. I'm really glad my parents chose it. I remember when I was young and I found out it was derived from Andrew and meant "mighty warrior," I would go around the house chanting, "Mighty warrior, mighty Andrea" in a sing-song voice probably to the annoyance of my siblings!

One website says, "This lovely name means 'strong', an essential quality to be a warrior." In my favourite baby naming book (from which we picked out our children's names) Andrea means 'womanly' and the bible verse to go with my name is Proverbs 31:28 ... "Her children arise and call her blessed; her husband also, and he praises her."

I have been mulling over Proverbs 31 quite a bit lately, as I finish writing this book. This section is probably more for women than men (sorry). Remembering back, when friends would send me verses on the Proverbs 31 woman, I never felt like I measured up to the standard mentioned in all those verses. But I am learning that it's not meant to be a checklist of unreachable goals, rather an example of the heart that I want to develop as God continues to work in my life.

I now believe these verses are not meant to shame us, make us feel like we're not good enough or highlight what we will never be; but they outline the attributes that we offer (as women) with unique and rich spiritual qualities. I was interested to learn that Jewish women set the spiritual atmosphere and tone for their home, making it into a divine spiritual place where souls flourish — serving God in all that they do. So even on the worst days when we feel like a failure, we are not failing if we are "fearing the Lord". And this beautiful picture of the Proverbs 31 woman who has her sense of 'self' grounded, not on superficial beauty or charm, but on her relationship with God — she sees these spiritual goals as what drives her.

Rabbi Danny Bergson said, "Time and time again when the Jewish people were faced with adversity (their existence threatened) it was the Jewish women that kept us going through their steadfast faith and trust in God." On Friday nights before the Shabbat meal, it's a tradition in some Jewish households for a husband to sing a song of praise to his wife called 'Eshet Chayil'.

The word 'chayil' is most commonly translated in English as "valor." We are women of valor! We are "noble," "forceful," "mighty," "excellent," "valiant," "brave" and "courageous." I love that! Out of the outpouring of God's love for you and an identity grounded and planted in Him, You can hold yourself up — and, if need be, others too — with strength.

Doesn't this redefine how you view yourself as a woman and even how you raise your daughters? I know that I want to raise my daughter to be strong, brave, and warrior-like in her faith and spiritual walk. I want her to be tenacious and bold. I want her to be a *'chayil'* woman — a woman of valor. I love this passage written by Luisa Rodriguez on the Proverbs 31 woman:

> *"So here is this king who most likely understands the warrior's heart. He receives a poem from his mother that refers to a highly praised woman as a valiant woman, as a chayil woman. Why? Because the intent is to get the king to appreciate this woman and her efforts to the same degree that he would value any mighty man of war. That what this woman does day in and day out is just as brave and valiant as a soldier in the midst of war. Ladies, if that doesn't give you goosebumps, I don't know what will. If you ever wondered if God notices what you do, reading Proverbs 31 should put that to rest. He wants men to see you and give you the same value that they would give their war brothers. God sees you, the woman that loves Him, that fights for her family, her church, her community, as valiant, and strong, and a warrior."*

In response to this, I declare that you are:

Steadfast, Brave, Trustworthy, Hardworking, Motivated, Faithful, Modest, A good steward of money and supplies, A helper to the poor, Compassionate towards others, Someone who opens her mouth carefully, Anointed with power to do the work of Jesus, Not afraid of what is outside your control, Prepared, Trusting in the Lord, Someone with good character and humility, Classy, Dignified, Wise, Kind, Smart, Savvy, Someone who contemplates eternity, a Mighty Warrior and ... (most importantly) someone who fears the Lord!

As I declare this list over my own life, it spurs me on all the more to keep developing and chasing these attributes. Not only were we fearfully and wonderfully made, but we were designed by God to bravely and faithfully give life to the world around us.

Final Words

It's really quite ironic because as I finish the last chapter of this book, the chapter of our family living here in Thailand is also coming to an end. I named this book 'No Fear of Winter' many, many years ago when I first began writing it. Now, I literally feel like those exact words are what I need to wash over me once again. As my family heads into the unknown, I am reminded that He has us! He is covering us. I love The Passion Translation in Psalm 91:4 where it says, "*His massive arms are wrapped around you protecting you. You can run under his covering of majesty and hide. His arms of faithfulness are a shield keeping you from harm.*"

Lately, I've been playing this song Oceans (Where Feet May Fail) a lot. It says:

> *"You call me out upon the waters*
> *The great unknown where feet may fail*
> *And there I find You in the mystery*

In oceans deep my faith will stand
And I will call upon Your name
And keep my eyes above the waves
When oceans rise
My soul will rest in Your embrace
For I am Yours and You are mine
Your grace abounds in deepest waters
Your sovereign hand will be my guide
Where feet may fail and fear surrounds me
You've never failed and You won't start now
So I will call upon Your name
And keep my eyes above the waves when oceans rise
My soul will rest in Your embrace
For I am Yours and You are mine
Spirit lead me where my trust is without borders
Let me walk upon the waters
Wherever You would call me
Take me deeper than my feet could ever wander
And my faith will be made."

While I was in the shower the other day, I felt God speak to my heart and say, *"The work is not done. It's only just begun. This is not the end ... it's just the beginning. The fight to end child trafficking within and through Australia starts now. You've been in training in Thailand and now you're taking all that you've learnt back to be a voice in an Australian context. But it's the same work."*

And so, I do not fear the unknown, for I know He is calling us and He is with us.

How will all this happen? I have so many questions. But as our pastor often tells us, "The world says, 'seeing is believing' but the Word says, 'believing is seeing.'"

I always need reminding that faith is the confidence that what I don't see or feel is real. In Romans 4:18 it says, "against all hope" or "against all odds" Abraham believed.

So, against all odds, I choose to believe. I wholeheartedly think that we will see breakthroughs in the child trafficking space, and that we can make a difference in this world to end it. I will keep trusting in God with all my heart (not my head) for our family through this next transition — leaning not on my own understanding.

I wrote back in the winter chapter that I have had times where I have felt His strong arms holding me; but I have also had to embrace moments of letting go, tearing down, grief, loss and uncertainty. I think these next few months will be a wintry one as we again say goodbye and grieve, but I know that when we arrive in Australia, it will literally be spring and figuratively speaking it will be as well; so we will see new beginnings and growth as the spring season bursts forth.

Why do I share these stories about my life and my family's journey so far? I think it's best explained when I reflect on John 4:39, "Many of the Samaritans from that town believed in him (Jesus) because of the woman's testimony ..."

It was *her story* which led them to meet Jesus, resulting in their belief and salvation. That struck me, because we all have a story. This lowly, outcast Samaritan woman was so moved by Jesus, that she sparked a revival in her neighbourhood! Each of us has the ability to impact others with our story. I do hope that whether you are a believer or not, that you will be encouraged by my testimony of God's faithfulness and love through every season.

ANDREA CROSS

Discussion Questions

Can you identify times in this season that reflect self-reliance, impatience or a resistance to being 'pruned'?

Are you using the spring as a time for personal growth and transformation? Reflect on your level of trust in God's faithfulness and timing.

"Even 'good' goodbyes can be difficult sometimes." Can you think of a time that this has been true in your life?

What small victories or personal growth can you identify in this season?

Have you made time to wander, explore or connect in a different way lately? How do you find it easiest to disconnect from the world and reconnect with God? What gets in the way of focusing on God?

How deep are you able to go with your friends, family and your own self-reflection at this time? Are you able to be honest and reflective in your reflections and relationships?

Are your family/ loved ones getting more than just your *scraps* of time? If not, what ideas can you think of that would improve the way you interact with those around you?

What are your deepest fears and inhibitions right now? What do you notice 'in your hand' that you are holding tight to? What needs to happen so that you can release it to God?

How does God see you? Do you know and understand His amazing love for you? Can you accept this free gift of love?

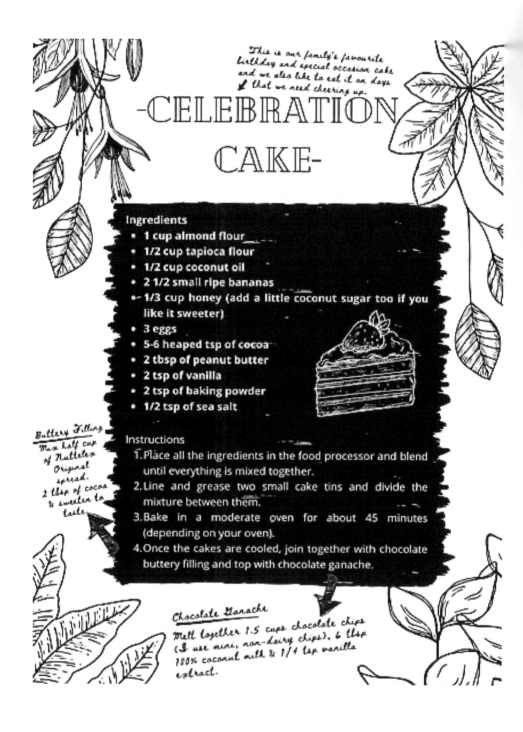

This is our family's favourite birthday and special occasion cake and we also like to eat it on days that we need cheering up.

-CELEBRATION CAKE-

Ingredients

- 1 cup almond flour
- 1/2 cup tapioca flour
- 1/2 cup coconut oil
- 2 1/2 small ripe bananas
- 1/3 cup honey (add a little coconut sugar too if you like it sweeter)
- 3 eggs
- 5-6 heaped tsp of cocoa
- 2 tbsp of peanut butter
- 2 tsp of vanilla
- 2 tsp of baking powder
- 1/2 tsp of sea salt

Instructions

1. Place all the ingredients in the food processor and blend until everything is mixed together.
2. Line and grease two small cake tins and divide the mixture between them.
3. Bake in a moderate oven for about 45 minutes (depending on your oven).
4. Once the cakes are cooled, join together with chocolate buttery filling and top with chocolate ganache.

Buttery Filling
Mix half cup of Nuttelex Original spread. 2 tbsp of cocoa & sweeten to taste.

Chocolate Ganache
Melt together 1.5 cups chocolate chips (I use mini, non-dairy chips). 6 tbsp 100% coconut milk & 1/4 tsp vanilla extract.

We love eating these pancakes on the weekends.

-SATURDAY'S PANCAKES-

This pancake mix is dairy free, refined sugar free and gluten free.

Ingredients

- 2-3 cups almond milk (depending on how thick you like your pancakes)
- 1 tsp vinegar
- 2 cups of gluten free flour
- 1 tsp baking soda
- ½ tsp salt
- 2 tbsp honey
- 2 eggs
- 2 tbsp coconut oil
- 1 tsp vanilla
- 1 ripe banana

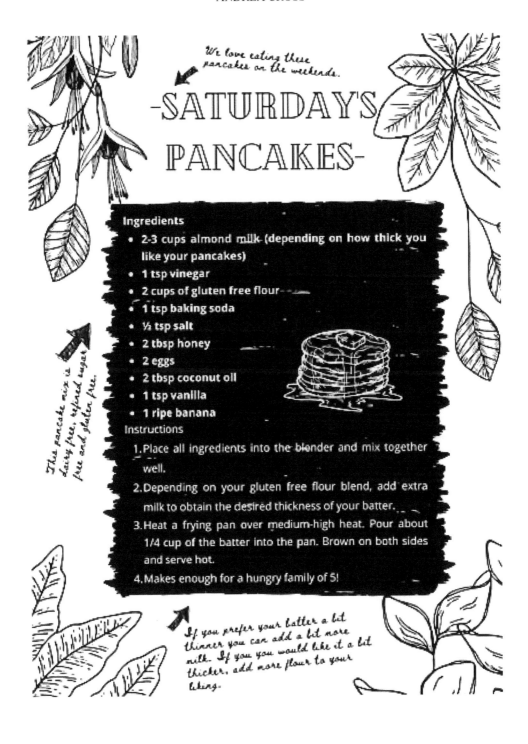

Instructions

1. Place all ingredients into the blender and mix together well.
2. Depending on your gluten free flour blend, add extra milk to obtain the desired thickness of your batter.
3. Heat a frying pan over medium-high heat. Pour about 1/4 cup of the batter into the pan. Brown on both sides and serve hot.
4. Makes enough for a hungry family of 5!

If you prefer your batter a bit thinner you can add a bit more milk. If you you would like it a bit thicker, add more flour to your liking.

A simple prayer to receive Jesus' free gift:

"Jesus, I invite You to come into my life and change my perspective on who You are.

Thank you for dying on the cross for me in order to bring me back into relationship with Father God.

Thank you for Your forgiveness.

I receive Your Holy Spirit now.

Thank you that You want me to be part of Your family.
AMEN"

If you have just prayed that prayer for the first or even the umpteenth time, then please talk to someone about what you have done. If you were given this book as a gift, talk to the person who gave it to you, or contact a local church for extra support to encourage you in your faith journey.

Editorial Postscript:

Andrea returned to Australia with her family in 2021 and continues to remain dedicated to fighting against the injustice of child trafficking. As her family transitions through various climatic and metaphorical life seasons — adapting back into a significantly different lifestyle and culture — Andrea has persisted in her work with the ZOE Foundation Australia. Together, they aim to build a community of individuals who are informed and educated about modern slavery. Andrea is particularly passionate about preventing child exploitation, rescuing children from danger, and seeing the restoration of every area of a child's life.

https://www.gozoe.org.au/